How
Personal Crisis
Can Enrich a
Woman's Life

THE CRITICAL MOMENT

Margaret Wold

AUGSBURG Publishing House
Minneapolis, Minnesota 55415

THE CRITICAL MOMENT

MANUFACTURED IN THE UNITED STATES OF AMERICA

CONTENTS

PREFACE

Each one of us has a crisis story to tell, a story about a critical moment that changed our life. That story is different from anyone else's story. In the years during which I've traveled this country—speaking, leading retreats, talking and working with groups of all kinds, but mostly with groups of women—I have been hearing those stories. On buses and planes, with little or no encouragement, passengers sitting next to me often revealed their personal pain as they related the circumstances of their lives.

Every time I leave town, I take the airport bus from the Disneyland Hotel to the Los Angeles International Airport. No sooner had I taken a vacant seat next to an attractive middle-aged woman on one of these journeys than she greeted me with the words, "You are now sitting next to one of those pathetic creatures who, after 34 years of marriage, is being divorced by her husband for a younger woman." During the hour-long ride, I listened to her tale of a troubled marriage to a physician, his many affairs through the years, their previous divorce and remarriage, and his current relationship with a nurse whom he was now going to marry. At the end of our ride, she said, "Why didn't I meet you a year ago? If only I had talked to someone then!"

At weekend retreats, women would come under cover of darkness to my assigned quarters, timid, tearful, often desperate, to pour out their stories of rejection, grief, anguish, self-loathing, guilt. Not always were they asking for help. Usually they just felt the need to share, to be listened to, and to know they were being heard.

Many would never come, fearing personal revelation and identification, or fearing that they might receive, instead of acceptance and the assurance of forgiveness and hope, a scolding or judgment. So I devised a personal "crisis questionnaire" which needed no signature but simply provided a structured method by means of which any woman who wanted to share her story could do so without fear of being personally identified. I would simply announce where the questionnaires could be found and invite any who wished to take them to do so and to return them to the same place upon completion. The results did not even need to be handed to me directly.

At first I wondered whether anyone would avail herself of this opportunity. So I was somewhat surprised when the three or four dozen questionnaires disappeared in an almost frantic stampede of individuals wanting them. There was always need for more forms, as word got around about this opportunity. Women were eager to share what they'd learned from their critical moments. Sometimes they would scribble on the questionnaire little phrases such as "Sharing makes the going easier." Another wrote, "Thanks, Marge, for giving me a chance to share this. I wish I could have done it years ago. It would have helped shorten the time it took me to get over it."

A young woman received this insight while writing: "Thanks for this opportunity. It's made me see that I am what I am and I have to live with myself and I want that life of mine to be in Christ. Thanks for letting me share the writing of my pain. I've come to see that I'm too possessive and clinging and I've tried to control the lives of those about me. That, I see now, is what's brought about my crisis. I think there's still time to change it all. Thanks for helping me to see."

Another confessed, "I really didn't want to pour all of this out, but I'm glad I did. It's become the most healing experience I've ever had. Thank you, thank you!" Some women asked to talk to me face to face after they had written it all down because they felt that they needed to experience a completion of the release they had begun to realize in the writing.

During a two-year period, I distributed my questionnaires at meetings from Alaska to South Dakota, from California to Montana. As I read the stories gathered, I discovered marvelous new insights into the nature of crisis. Each story was so personal to its owner, yet all of them contained so much that was common.

The earliest crisis story occurred when its writer was age 10, the latest one at age 73. Out of the hundreds collected, I selected 100 of the most complete and open accounts. Under assumed names, the women who lived those stories will tell them to you in the pages that follow. For you, the reader, this book will provide an opportunity to think through your own crisis story, to examine what you learned from it, and to affirm again the strengths that developed as a result.

In the first chapter, the description of many critical

moments may revive some long-buried or freshly experienced pain. As one woman wrote, "Just to write my story again has brought tears and reopened wounds. But it's releasing to share the agony with someone besides God." As you continue to work your way through the chapters, I am convinced that you will experience the healing of memories and emotions that you may long have denied and which, unexpressed, may be preventing your recovery from pain and despair.

The stories were shared as a gift from the many women to whom they belong in the expressed hope that their sharing will be helpful to you. God's Word assures them that this will happen. "Our hope for you is unshaken; for we know that as you share in our sufferings, you will also share in our comfort" (2 Cor. 1:7).

But beyond the sharing and beyond the comfort, yes, beyond *your* critical moment, lie power and strength. If you have not yet found that power and strength for yourself, accept this book as a step toward discovery.

The human body may be incredibly fragile and the human mind seems to walk a precarious tightrope between sanity and insanity, but I have come to respect the human spirit as incredibly tough as it opens itself to the power available from its Creator, Redeemer, and Counselor.

I believe that the road to that discovery passes through crisis. The stories in this book support that belief.

God bless your reading.

1

THE MOMENT THAT CHANGES LIFE

Critical moments come equipped with taloned claws, tearing time itself into raggedly bleeding pieces of before and after. Life will never again assume its former shape.

The moments take many forms. A skiing accident breaks both her ankles and a young woman's husband announces, "I never intended to be married to a cripple," and walks out.

The telephone rings and a mother hears, "This is the FBI, and we're calling to tell you that we've picked up your son. He's charged with conspiring to bomb government installations."

For 22-year-old Marta, crisis was a slow-motion nightmare of deep depression in which she was unable to control her actions. One day she was arrested and jailed for stealing. Nausea returns with every memory of that day.

During those ten hours in a prison cell, I was in the bottom of a hole. I thought I would never get to the top and I was close to suicide. My life was ruined and things would never be bright again. I was numb and sick to my stomach at the same time and completely without the desire to fight. I was alone, locked up for 10 hours of hell. No one answered my screams. I felt depraved, stripped naked in front of those I loved. I wished I'd die.

In Julie's crisis, blood was pouring out of her faster than transfusions could replace it. How does a 20-year-old girl with ulcerative colitis make the decision to have an ileostomy?* The doctor's words were decisive: "It's either have this operation or you'll die. There's nothing more I can do for you except surgery." "Oh, my God, no!" Her conviction was that God was picking on her. "Why me? I'm only 20 years old! Many people go through their whole life without having to come face-to-face with a decision like this!" Death seemed preferable to the loss of all she had been and would never be again once the operation took place.

When Helen was told that their second son was born "severely brain damaged, unable to move, no reflexes, the walls of my life closed in on all sides," and she screamed against the cruel fate that irreparably trapped both her and the baby.

Annie will never forget that cold January day when her husband told her that he was in love with the wife of his best friend. For Annie the shock was intensified by the close social ties which had bound both couples. They were frequent guests in each other's homes and the woman had appeared to be Annie's friend, too. "I

---

* The operation creating an artificial opening through the abdominal wall into the intestine.

couldn't believe this was happening to me and my family. I felt like I was living a nightmare. Despair, sadness flooded me. I wanted to run and run and run."

Numb with fright, 28-year-old Lisa heard the police officer telling her over the phone that her husband had "gone berserk" at work and had been forcibly taken to a psychiatric ward. The days that followed are still part of her nightmares.

> For some time I had been aware that things were somehow very wrong with him but, having been taught to be a "good" wife and mother and never to complain no matter what my husband did, I didn't know where to turn. My husband had almost convinced me that I was the one who was crazy. When I arrived at the hospital the doctor said it was up to my husband whether he stayed there or came home; so he came home. We arranged for help when I went to work but he wouldn't cooperate with psychiatric appointments or take his medication. Everything went along for a while and then there was another breakdown, this time while he was in Sunday school. Eight months later my husband was killed in a one-car accident. My nightmares have lasted for years and during the daytime I have moments even now when I panic.

Katie's crisis was compounded by guilt. Very ill with a severe throat infection, she asked her nine-year-old daughter to look in the medicine basket for throat lozenges. When the girl brought the lozenges to Katie, she left the basket on a low shelf within reach of two-year-old Cindy. A little later, Cindy came into the living room where Katie lay on the couch and proudly announced, "I took some medicine for my sore throat, too."

The sight of the white powder on her lips and on her

13

tongue quickened Katie's heartbeat into violent pounding.

> I tried to be very casual when I asked my husband to see what she had gotten into, not knowing that the medicine basket was within her reach. Minutes later when she couldn't answer my questions, I discovered that the only really harmful medication in the basket —a narcotic for facial nerve pain—was empty. A wave of dizziness swept over me, and I grabbed her and jammed my finger down her throat and made her vomit. Outside a blinding blizzard had drifted in our driveway. The agonizing walk to a neighbor's house and the long drive to the hospital through the drifted snow was a nightmare of slow motion. All the way there and all the time I sat next to her was like a visit to hell. How could I, a nurse, have kept that medicine? Now my child was delirious. She might die. The hospital sent me home with my flu and sore throat and fever. I couldn't even stay with her. I could never forgive myself!

Nora's nightmares still wake her up hearing over and over again the same voice that woke her so many months before.

> When I opened my eyes there stood a tall man with a gun against my face. He told me to lie on the floor with my husband and parents. I heard him going through the entire house, taking all monies and jewelry. He even came over to where I lay shaking and pulled off the wedding band and the diamond which had been mine for 30 years. He took everything of value in the house including our drivers' licenses, with the threat of harm in the event he was arrested. There was no doubt in our minds that he meant to use the gun if we tried to scream or fight against him. I don't know if I will ever be able to

14

sleep with the lights off or stay alone in the house at night again.

Crisis is no respecter of age, striking young and old alike. Wendy was only 10 when part of her died. We like to think that "children get over things faster than adults do," but it took Wendy nearly 10 years to get over the fact that she would never again see her best friend, who moved away because her father was caught stealing money from the mail. "The town was small and new people did not move into it so I had little chance of replacing her. Whenever I saw groups of children laughing and playing together, I would run away and cry, unable to accept the fact that I would have to survive without Linda."

The wounds were still fresh enough to bring a flood of tears when Sherri told me that just a month before her brother-in-law had come to visit and had told her, "Last night your husband took me to meet his new girl friend. He just doesn't love you anymore, Sherri. He's been going out with other women for a couple of years and he has a whole group of friends that you don't know at all. They're into smoking pot and he brags about getting away with what he's doing without your knowing about it."

"I can't get over crying. My whole world has gone to pieces," Sherri sobbed. "I've searched my soul and prayed. I don't know what I could have done differently. I thought we were getting along all right. It's such a shock!"

Divorce claims more marriages every year. For many women it comes as a devastating crisis. Tina was 38 when her husband told her that he was in love with someone else. "My husband said he felt like life was passing him by. It was almost as if he felt compelled to have an affair. I held on for a while, trying to hold our marriage together, but finally decided on the divorce because my heart was breaking. A year later I still felt lost; he was my whole life and living for him had been my greatest joy. Now mornings and sunsets are unbearable times. They mean I have to face another day and another night without him."

Jane, at 27, had been married eight years and had a beautiful two-year-old adopted son. Every day they expected a call from the adoption agency telling them that they had a little girl.

> Instead I got a phone call at six P.M. from my husband saying that he did not love me anymore and wanted to end our marriage. I couldn't believe it! We had dated all through school. He was brilliant, happy-go-lucky, and we seemed to get along so well. We were both so thrilled with our new little son and had built a lovely home. We attended the same church but the last year of our marriage was tough. He began to drink heavily, gambled a lot, and then I got the phone call. Why was it that I didn't see what was happening? He married his secretary a few months later. The hurt was immense. I love him and I had tried so hard to be a good and loving wife and mother. I did everything I could think of. I told him I'd do anything to have him back but his mind was made up.

It's possible that Americans are more preoccupied with all aspects of marriage than are any other people in the world. The role of wife is still central for many women in the United States, despite the fact that many of them have satisfying careers also. So relationships with husbands and children figure largely in the critical moments described by women.

Nearly 95% of all Americans will be married at least once before they die, a fact which makes American marriage rates among the highest in the world. In books, television, and movies we devote a great deal of space and energy to examining all areas of the marriage relationship and of divorce, dissecting the roles, frustrations, and adjustments.

Since in the United States marriage means two people living together in one household with a high degree of intimacy and sharing, the dissolution of that relationship may be much more personally traumatic than in cultures in which extended families are common.

When marriage carries the heavy weight of need for romance and personal fulfillment, it is difficult to meet its demands. Since hopes for the relationship are so high, any inability to live up to those expectations tends to be looked on as failure and becomes a reason for looking for a mate who seems better qualified to fill the expectations. While some marriages return from the brink of divorce with satisfactory results, in many cases this does not happen.

So the search for the "perfect mate" goes on, leaving in its wake a trail of broken dreams. Strangely enough, then, divorce evidently does not imply disillusionment with marriage in general, since the remarriage rate of the divorced is very high. Instead it may indicate the impossibility of living up to the impossible demands modern marriage makes on both partners.

Our society appears to be in a stage of transition to greater permissiveness concerning divorce, removing the stigma of failure, rejection, and great social disgrace it once bore. Nevertheless, by far the greatest number of women I interviewed identified divorce as their greatest crisis.

Occasionally divorce brought not crisis but relief.

For Marie the thought of being single and alone after 25 years of marriage was frightening. But the moment of crisis for her came when she made her own decision to divorce a husband who told her he did not love her, who ridiculed her, made fun of her, degraded her with every word, and who openly and unashamedly spent all waking hours with another woman. He enjoyed admitting that he committed adultery, apparently delighting in the hurt he saw in Marie. For a woman who had been taught from earliest years that marriage was "'til death do us part," it was tough to make the decision to divorce. Only years of prayer and counseling from a Christian pastor gave her the strength.

While divorce may strike more deeply at feelings of self-worth, death of a spouse is final. Never easy to cope with under any circumstances or at any age, the number of scars it leaves seems to be related to the degree of happiness and freedom in the marriage.

Dody's husband was killed in a racing car accident less than two months after they had purchased a new business.

> Even though I felt all alone and abandoned and wondered why I was left to deal with all the work, I felt no guilt. I had been told by my husband many times that he could never find another wife like me. My anger at times makes up for my lack of guilt and I feel just mad at the world! But I have no regrets. We loved each other and we had a good marriage at the time of his death. We did what we wanted to do, and in the 35 years he lived he had done as much and lived as fully as a man of 70. There are no changes that could have been made to make life better. My husband died doing what he loved best —racing—and he would not have wanted to live maimed. He enjoyed the active life too much and neither one of us would want it any other way.

When Janice's husband of 21 years died within 24 hours of a cerebral hemorrhage, she was left with four teenagers to care for. "I wasn't prepared," she writes. "I'd never lost anyone I loved in death before that time and I had to read of other women's experiences to know that my feelings of depression and fear of the future were normal."

Marion remembers every minute of that "last" day.

My husband Hank kissed me good-bye at 7:10 A.M. on January 23, perfectly well. He walked one block and dropped dead. He had asked me to take him to work that day but I begged off because I had some Bible reading to do for a class. When the medical examiner came to tell me, I told him I needed a minute to think. I went off by myself and thanked God for 32 years of marriage and for taking Hank fast because he was scared to death of doctors. I never had a down moment. We had had a good life together.

While the number of surviving husbands has remained fairly constant in the past 50 years, widows have increased significantly in number. Widows outnumber widowers past age 65 by about five to one. A widow lives longer alone (18 years average) following the death of her husband than the widower does after his wife's death (13 years). Today the average age at which women become widows is in the mid-fifties.

The role of widow may be more difficult to adjust to than the role of widower for several reasons. In American society the marriage relationship is usually more important to the woman than the man and the end of marriage means ending a role more basic to a surviving woman than to a surviving man. Also there are fewer opportunities for a woman to remarry than for a man, not only because of the shorter life expectancy of men, but also because widowers tend to marry women several years younger than themselves. The widow's financial potential is usually less than that of the widower. Combined with the fact that she has been socially trained to be less aggressive, this forces her into a more restricted social life than that of a widower.

The most common problem for a widow is loneliness, especially for women who live in the city. In any given age group, widows have a higher suicide rate than married women of the same age, especially widows who had been extremely dependent on their husbands. It's no wonder that the death of a husband is one of the most severe crises women experience.

For women who are mothers, the death of a child is catastrophic. Looking back across the years to the death of her two little ones—a 3-year-old girl and an 18-month-old boy—within a week of each other, Esther still wonders how she survived. "I remember standing at the kitchen sink about a month after the second funeral," she said, "and I thought I heard a voice coming from behind me right over my shoulder saying, 'Why don't you kill yourself? You don't have anything to live for now, do you?' The temptation was so strong. I started shaking like a leaf. All I could say was, 'In the name of Jesus, leave me alone!'"

In *Love and Will* Rollo May says that the "relationship between love and death is perhaps the most clear to people when they have children" (p. 100). No one is more vulnerable to the terrifying loss by death than those who have nurtured a child.

So for Ruth the sudden accidental death of her first-born, an 18-year-old son on whom she was very dependent, was a violent experience. "I never realized that losing a loved one in death could be so painful! I just couldn't breathe when I got the news. The next thing I remember was pounding the table with clenched hands and crying out to God, 'Please don't let it be real!' "

As you read these stories poured out of the hearts of other women, what do you feel? Sympathy, judgment, pain? We often read news stories and think, "These are things that happen to *other* people." Then one day the news story is about *us* or someone we love; the failure of *our* marriage has become public record, or that terse obituary is the public notice that part of us has left this earth forever. Then the fantasies all become reality and like Ruth we scream, "Please, God, don't let it be real!"

All the statistics so casually read by millions of us every day—one out of so many will die in auto accidents over the holiday weekend, says the newscaster—in one split second the impersonal statistic becomes our personal biography.

All those events and happenings that so swiftly change the course of our lives, those things that happen *to* us, from outside of ourselves—I call them *crises of happening*.

The reason a crisis of happening is so devastating is that we're never prepared for it, no matter how many warnings we're given. "One out of so many will die of lung cancer if they smoke for so many years at the rate of so many packages a day." Statistic. Will I be one of the "ones" or one of the "others"? Consciously I know that I have a good possibility of being a "one" but my psyche persuades me to deny that as a possibility for myself and encourages me to believe that I will be one of the lucky statistics.

I live in California and like millions of others I've heard repeated warnings of a disastrous earthquake. So I've posted a card with the list of "What to Do When an Earthquake Comes" in the kitchen. Predictions say that thousands of us will die in that quake, but I simply do not believe that I will be one of them.

Many women report denying crises of happening for days, weeks, and even years after they happen. "It seems like a dream," they say, "and every day I have to tell myself that it really happened."

Other crises occur simply because, from the time we are born, we are in the process of aging. These are *crises of growing*. A popular explorer of adult "maturational" crises is Gail Sheehy, whose book *Passages* hit the best-seller market with an impact that demonstrates forcefully how accurately she has described crisis as a normal feature of the developmental process.

Aging occurs not only in people over 65. Aging is happening all the time to all of us. In that process changes occur in our bodies, our minds, and our perceptions of ourselves and of the world. Daily we are coming closer to death. "One out of one dies." No "other" percentages are operative. Awareness of that final reality penetrates every level of conscious, every unconscious thought.

Susan describes her own crisis of growing—her own unique experience, but one which strikes familiar chords in the spirits of those of us who have lived to tell it.

> Seven years ago I "cracked up," with all the complications, the panic, and the pain that follow—the naked truth that must be revealed to parents who are already upset. The following year I was healed of a minor case of schizophrenia (if there is such a thing!). It was all so unexpected. I was going along in a way that I thought was the way of a normal teenager when all of a sudden out of some hidden part of my being came a cry and a panic and a need that I didn't even recognize as part of me. That was when I tried to commit suicide and failed miserably (praise the Lord!), but I don't want to describe it

any further because it's too painful to dredge up that part of my past that I've worked so hard to heal.

At the heart of all of our crises of growing is an anxiety that is born along with us at the time of our birth. Shocked by our entry into a cold and hostile environment from the warm comfort of the womb, we develop, along with the cutting of the umbilical cord and that first slap on the bottom, what the late great psychiatrist Karen Horney calls our "basic anxiety."

Every moment of our life, each new situation provides fertile soil for that anxiety to develop into a full-blown crisis. Each unknown circumstance, every strange new feeling stirring out of the subconscious, any evidence of strange behavior on the part of others or of myself can trigger that basic fear, the fear that I might be abandoned, alone, left without support in an unfriendly and hostile world. Every day of my life, dependence and the longing for someone to take care of me fights with my desire to be free, independent, and autonomous.

Seesawing between both needs, I am often out of equilibrium. When I am able to satisfy both my dependency needs and my longings for independence, then I feel good and equilibrium is restored. But we walk a fragile and precarious tightrope and there are forces within and without that constantly push at this delicate state. So if I lose my job, get sick or divorced, or a loved one dies; if I flunk a test, fail a course, don't get enough sleep, or take drugs that throw me off balance—any one of these can trigger that basic anxiety which is always there to produce a crisis reaction.

More basic than the crisis of happening (situational) or the crisis of growing (maturational) is the *crisis of being* (identity).

"Who am I?" is a question that can bring a different answer every day. Today I am not the same person that I was yesterday or that I will be tomorrow. But the question assumes more significance at certain times than it does at others, because it's closely tied to our roles. When we are making the transition from one role to another, in that period between losing one role identity and finding another, we experience a crisis of being.

For instance, in adolescence I am casting off my child role but still do not have an adult role. "Who am I?" In the midyears, I am no longer a young person but neither am I old. So if I do some of the things I used to do I may find myself unacceptable in a younger group which now identifies those activities as its own, but I may not be ready to give them up and yield to the injunction to act my age. So, "Who am I?"

If I lose my job and my identity as "teacher," "counselor," "boss," and stay at home, who am I? Or if I retire and join an older adult community where nobody knows me by my former roles, who am I? How will I find a new identity?

As our whole sense of being crumbles, we may experience a crisis of being during the period of reconstruction before a new identity is established. A crisis of this nature is closely related to both other types and may be triggered by one or the other.

The positive aspect of the crisis of being is that it gives us an opportunity to search for newness. After all, not everything about that old "me" may have been good!

It could be that I didn't like the hurried, rushed, preoccupied person my former roles forced me to be. Maybe I'd rather not be known by roles at all, but as "that person who's so warm and relaxed"; or as "the woman who plays tennis" instead of as "the woman who always has a spotless house." Maybe instead of being known as "the busy lawyer's wife" I'd like to have a new identity as "the woman who's fun to be around." Perhaps I would rather shed the A-student identity for a good-friend reputation. Changing times and opportunities to travel may have changed me from a conservative to a more liberal view of things and I need new activities that reflect my new attitudes.

This crisis period will come between leaving friends who are associated with the former activities and before finding new friends and groups who affirm me in my new identity. That feeling of not belonging anywhere, of being in limbo, brings to the surface basic anxiety and the dread sense of abandonment.

And in all of the crises described in this chapter, whether of happening, growing, or being, that experience of total aloneness becomes the "horror at the bottom."

Something to think about

1. How old were you when your "crisis" occurred?
2. Tell the story of your crisis. Write it here and on the next pages.

Continue your story here. Let it become part of this book just as the other stories in this chapter have become part of it.

2

THE HORROR AT THE BOTTOM

I don't know how else to describe my reaction. I felt like I was going to pieces. I heard myself scream-ing and crying behind the closed doors of my room, and yet when I was with people, I felt icy and numb and completely worthless. Thoughts of suicide were almost constantly under every conscious thought and I felt like hurting someone as much as I had been hurt. I broke furniture and tried to take a bottle of aspirin. I tried to cut myself on the arms and legs with a knife. I became very antisocial and hostile, totally destructive. Sometimes when I was driving along the road and would see a person or two walk-ing along the side, I would think it would be fun just to drive into them and kill them. If I couldn't be happy, I didn't want anyone to be happy.

Linnie, a highly competent professional woman, paints her feelings in vivid colors and with bold outlines. While her actions are violent and often out of control, Linnie is not alone in her feelings. Every one of the emotions she describes was also described by other women in their stories. Linnie's story is unique in that she acted on her feelings in ways that were often threatening to other people, and it was this that drove Linnie to seek professional help.

Unless we are dead or in certain psychotic states, we *feel.* Even when we describe ourselves as "icy and numb," we are describing a feeling. In times of stress feelings can become so tumultuous that it's not at all strange to feel "icy and numb" and at the same time experience a feeling of being "continually scalded by boiling water," as Linnie says she did.

This battle within was described by women in terms of extreme conflict: "I wanted to die but everything in me fought to live." "I was laughing and crying and I didn't know why I did either one." "I was praying, but all the time I was feeling that God was very distant." "I felt that God was with me but like he was on vacation." "I felt more awake than I had ever felt in my life and yet it was like walking through a dream."

Even under the best of circumstances people often have a tough time coping with life. I don't know from firsthand experience what it was like to live in another age, but I do know from firsthand experience that life in the 20th century is full of stress. It takes a strong person with a fairly secure childhood and a high degree of adaptability just to keep up with the rapidly changing world in which we live. Add to that the bombardment by all kinds of stimuli so much of the time and it's no wonder that at least 50,000 people each year in the United States decide that life isn't worth the struggle and kill themselves. Most of them are in good health, but apparently come to the conclusion that death is better than life. We say that they couldn't *cope*.

Pete was a very smart college student when I met him some years ago in a class at the University of North Dakota. He came from a good stable farm family, was good-looking and had a girl friend, and got good grades. But right before Christmas vacation, he put a gun to his head and shot himself. The note he left told his parents not to blame themselves, but he felt "so lonely that I can't stand to live anymore." Something in what Pete was *feeling* was more powerful than all the other seemingly good things he had going for him.

Now add to all the other pressures on our lives a time of severe crisis and it's not hard to see why our emotions go into a tailspin. Such basic ingredients for happiness as our needs for love, a sense of worth, and fun are the first to go in crisis. Take, for instance, the woman who is divorced. Does she feel loved? What about her sense of worth? And what happens to the fun in her life? What's left is rage, despair, guilt, and a sense of abandonment.

In one way or another feelings must be dealt with. In its own way denial of feelings is as destructive as Linnie's acting them out, because repressed feelings may surface as depression, psychosis, or illness, and all of these expressions may cause further crises. Linnie's actions could have resulted in criminal charges and ultimate imprisonment; depression ruins interpersonal relationships; psychosis or "craziness" sends one to asylums; and illness destroys our bodies and also works hardships on families.

Since feelings will "out," our society, including Christians, seems to have selected psychosomatic illness as its "symptom of choice." Estimates of the frequency of such illnesses run as high as 75% of the cases in doctors' offices. Psychosomatic (mind/body) illness is a 20th century term, but long before that doctors were prescribing ocean voyages to cure depression, not only for the rest involved but because breathing salt air would lift the spirits. Which one of us, when under stress, has not experienced loss of appetite or its opposite—compulsive, "nervous" eating?

Some people release emotional energy in enormous bursts of physical activity, tearing the house apart in a flurry of housecleaning, writing letters furiously, or attacking the garden with murderous intent toward all weeds, pests, and recalcitrant hedges! Other normally active people find themselves wanting to rest all day and are tired constantly, even after 9 and 10 hours of sleep. Linnie's behavior was socially unacceptable simply because her need to deal with her violent anger against a lover who had "jilted" her was released toward others. When this kind of "acting out" behavior is chosen as a way of release, the person is more likely to be defined as emotionally ill.

Psychosomatic illness is violence against one's own body, and while it may keep one out of jails and psychiatric hospitals, it sentences one to years of sitting in doctors' offices, paying medical bills, and undergoing needless tests and examinations to find out that there isn't anything physically wrong.

Feelings unexpressed push one down deeper into the pit of despair. Talking about them is the best way of siphoning them off before they become destructive, but too often there's no one to talk to.

When Jill looks back on her boyfriend's drowning in her 15th year, she says wistfully, "I wish I could have talked to his and my friends about our feelings concerning death, but we were all just silent. That's what made it so hard. Why didn't we even talk about it in the family? It seems that death and sex were subjects we always avoided."

Lori looks back on her needs at the time her 24-year-old son was killed in a car accident and says, "I could have used much more sharing. I had such a need to talk! I longed for friends to visit in the weeks following the funeral but nobody seemed to want to talk about my feelings. We were all in a conspiracy to avoid talking. But what do you do with your feelings when nobody wants you to express them?"

The urgency of that need comes through in the passionate words of another woman when I asked what she would do differently if she could live through her crisis time again: "I would yell, scream, and beg for someone to talk to me—anyone!"

Betty believes she could have avoided a breakdown after the death of her husband if she had had "some really close person that I could have shared everything with. Even though I was a Christian and the Holy Spirit ministered to my needs in wonderful ways which sustained me through the crisis, it was afterwards that the need for people surfaced and there just wasn't anybody who seemed to want to listen. As I look back I think I probably should have gone to a counselor because it would have helped me know more about my feelings and why I felt the way I did."

Over and over again the longing for "more adults to talk to about my feelings" cries out from the pages of writing, no matter what the age of the writer or the circumstances of her crisis.

And my mother used to say, "You talk too much to people!" But I was looking for something, *someone* to help me. Where were all these people you see in movies or read about in stories? Those sages, wise men and women, who can sit down and with a few simple words settle everything for you. *Where were all of these people when I needed them?*

Why have we become a people who cannot listen to each other's pain? Is it because we can't stand our own pain? Are we reluctant to take the time necessary for empathetic listening? Are we just too absorbed in coping with our own problems? Do we have nothing (or feel we have nothing) to contribute to the sufferer?

Perhaps we hold back because we have grown up with the idea that we have to "do something" about other people's problems, to be "problem-solvers," and if we can't offer a solution, we are afraid of our own sense of failure. But problem-solvers do not seem to be what's needed. Women long simply for someone to listen, to care, to not shy away from exploring feelings which are tearing them apart.

The pleading cry is simply, "Will you be my friend? Will you walk with me just a little way, feel what I am feeling, experience what I'm experiencing, and, by sharing my suffering for just a little while, make it less painful?" So crucial is this need that we are devoting an entire chapter of this book to "the circle of lovers."

Unless feelings can be expressed verbally and accepted without judgment, they find their own channels for expression. Linnie felt that she couldn't talk about her crisis, and antisocial behavior was the result.

> A hoped-for engagement cooled off. I was gradually rejected by my lover. This actually went on for five nightmarish years during which all hope for marriage with this man I loved, all hope for children was extinguished. I had known him for 10 years when he told me, "I don't love you anymore. I can't even bear to call you by an endearing name." I was 33 years old and it was an experience of such complete personal humiliation that I even moved to another

country. I felt that I had to get out of the United States and never again meet anyone that I had known before. I was rejected, unloved, a spinster, and everything in my whole small-town background said that was like being a leper in the Bible—unclean, unwanted, *alone*.

In Linnie's town the social climate made it impossible to talk about her feelings. How could she verbalize those feelings when she perceived herself as being completely undesirable socially? Fear of social rejection in addition to her personal rejection sealed her lips.

To have to pretend that you are not rejected, that you don't feel humiliated, that everything's okay and under control puts unbearable pressure on the human mind and body.

Even though feelings may be denied, the body is aware of them, and that's why psychosomatic illness has become common in our sealed-lip world. Our autonomic nervous system, outside of our voluntary control, reacts even when we keep outward expression of those feelings bottled up. The entire gamut of psychosomatic illnesses may be autonomic expressions—a tightened stomach, a throbbing head, intestinal spasms, elevated blood pressure, heart pains, lower back muscle spasms.

As a pastor's wife, Monica was convinced that she had to hide her feelings. She assumed that Christian leaders must always be (or appear to be) strong and above those human feelings of weakness which were the prerogative of lesser mortals.

After all I had gone through, I still fight a strong message not to tell others about my feelings. If I do, I feel guilty and ashamed, but what a cost there has been to my own self, to my family, to my husband, to my friends! I just could not communicate what I was going through to others whom, I felt, would not take kindly such feelings in a pastor's wife. And especially I felt that I couldn't talk to my husband who expected me to be his great "helpmate"! I could just yell and hurt inside.

Between the times of feeling like screaming were the other times when I wanted to curl up and die and disappear. I felt a failure as a mother because I was screaming at my four children. I felt a failure as a wife because I certainly was not bringing any happiness to my spouse. But most of all I was a failure, I felt, as a person because I was not what God wanted me to be. I couldn't be the perfect pastor's wife; instead I was a screaming witch, out of control in my bitchiness. My shoulders ached from the weight of it all. *I had great physical pain and many illnesses.*

For five years I pushed it all down and tried to be what I thought I ought to be. Dear God, how I tried! When I couldn't hold it in any longer, I just fell to pieces.

Then I had to open up and pour out all the feelings, but that was the beginning of my healing.

Monica tried so hard to push all of her feelings down, to deny them, to live as though she were without human emotions. But our emotions may be the most real thing about us. Our behavior is motivated by our feelings; with our minds we intellectualize and justify the behavior that comes from those feelings. So Monica's emotions would not be denied and came out in her screaming "bitchy" behavior, in her aching shoulders and her physical pain and illness. The tighter she pushed the lid down on her feelings, the more they boiled and churned and built up such great pressure within her psyche that finally there was just not enough strength in her to push the lid down any longer and an explosion almost destroyed her.

Both Monica and Linnie are victims of social pressures which denied them the right to express their feelings. Whether those social pressures really exist or are simply perceived, they are real to the person experiencing them and they effectively block the free expression of feeling.

Following the ocean accident which broke my husband's neck and paralyzed him for many months, it took me three years to learn the importance of not denying one's feelings during times of stress. Throughout his hospital stay Erling was crying freely and unashamedly for the first time in his life, and God only knows how much that had to do with hastening his miraculous recovery! But people have always told me that I am "strong," and I believed them and tried to live up to their expectations. As a result, I never permitted myself to grieve, to let go and cry it all out. Every time my feelings surfaced I'd tell myself, "Come on, stop feeling sorry for yourself! Self-pity is unproductive. You're a strong person. Think positive! Don't give in to weakness!" Can you hear yourself saying the same thing in a crisis?

God *was* present with me, and I truly *did* experience joy through all the pain we went through (and to some extent are still going through), but I did not understand that tears and outward expression of feelings are God-given safety valves in times of stress. People who don't cry (like "big" girls and boys?) are much more prone to stress-related illnesses than those who release their feelings through tears. Tears don't necessarily mean that one is sad and without hope; they just release strong emotion. Joyful occasions may produce as many tears as do sad ones. I thought I understood this, but somehow I didn't believe it.

There were many pressures after Erling's accident.

Suddenly I had to support the family. We moved to a new city, and I started a new job. I was doing all the things Erling could no longer do. All of this busyness further conspired to push my own emotional needs down below conscious awareness.

Writing about the experience in our two books (*What Do I Have to Do—Break My Neck?* and *Thanks for the Mountain,* Augsburg Publishing House, Minneapolis) was therapeutic, but the therapy took place on a mental rather than an emotional level. It's difficult to become deeply emotional when you're thinking about sentence construction, action verbs, and punctuation marks! So I talked and wrote about my feelings, but I didn't permit myself to *feel.*

Three years after the accident I was enrolled in a summer counseling workshop. During a small group session, one of the group members said that he was unable to trust other people. The group leader suggested an exercise to help him experience trust. He asked the man, whose name was John, to lie on the floor. Then he asked other members of the group to place their hands under John's body, to lift him carefully, and, cradling him in their arms, to rock him gently.

I started to participate with the rest of the group when, to my surprise, the exercise ceased to be role-playing for me. I found myself carried back to that August afternoon at Laguna Beach three years before. I was reliving the critical moment when we lifted Erling's paralyzed body out of the salt waters of the Pacific and carried him so very carefully to higher ground to wait for the ambulance.

I could not go on with the exercise. I sat down on the floor, fighting the pressure of tears pushing up hard from somewhere way down deep in my stomach. I tried to blot out that ocean scene by focusing on a doorknob, on a fly buzzing nearby—anything to deny the emotion that was boiling up inside me. I was afraid that I was going to "make a fool of myself."

It was no use. As the group in the classroom continued to rock John's body, I started to sob—great racking, unladylike sobs that echoed in the hushed room. While the group laid John's body gently down on the floor, I cried until there were no sobs left. No one tried to stop me; I sensed a quiet acceptance of my need to cry. The person next to me touched me gently on my shoulder but no one moved to cut my pain short.

During the two weeks we had been together, I had not told the group about Erling's accident. After I stopped crying, I started to talk. I realized that, while I had apparently convinced myself that I had no need to cry about what had happened in our lives, that denial had not convinced my subconscious mind. There the tears lay buried in a very shallow grave of memory, waiting for just the right moment to be resurrected as the grief they were meant to be.

The healing effect of that moment released me from the need to deny my feelings. I had revealed my feared "weakness" and no one had judged me for it. Instead of criticism, I received love and acceptance. This freed me from pretending to be something other than human, a cut above the "average" person who expressed feelings normal to crisis and grief. How freeing not to have to hold such a tight rein on my emotions!

I believe, from years of listening to the stories of other women, that many others are being "brave" in much the same way I was being brave. They have tucked all of that unexpressed grief and unshared experience deep down inside themselves, where it keeps growing and causing pressure like a great big tumor of pain.

Among all the emotions experienced during crisis,

none brings more pain and distress than the one which was identified five times more than any other feeling by those women who shared their lives with me.

"I felt all alone, abandoned, forsaken!"

Can you hear that barely whispered scream of Jesus, "My God, my God, why have you forsaken me?"

That may be what crisis is all about. *Any experience that forces an individual to feel that sense of lonely isolation and complete abandonment is a crisis.*

Without knowing that they are describing the "basic anxiety" Karen Horney defined, women tell how it feels to experience that abandonment, that sense of being all alone in a world where no one seems to understand or care, where no one reaches out to you and where you refuse to reach out to others.

Under the compulsion of that lost loneliness, one woman writes, "I hurt, so I walked and walked and cried out loud. Every sunset for days I walked alone and cried." Another says, "I just went into hiding. I didn't want to talk to anyone, family, friends, or neighbors. I was completely alone. I could get through the day but as soon as the sun went down, so did I." Or as someone else describes her reaction to the pain of abandonment, "I wanted to build a wall around my family and myself and then I felt we could never be hurt again."

Why do some of us scream and fight and attack others when we are in pain while others just keep crying inside? Do we have characteristic ways of behaving which operate almost automatically to control our actions when we are under pressure?

Apparently there is evidence to support this theory, but given the premise that we are unique individuals in the constant process of growing and changing, there are no sure and set ways of predicting how we're going to feel or behave when a crisis comes. Feelings surface which completely surprise us and we need new ways of coping with them.

In all cases it's essential to identify our feelings, to have them recognized as "normal," and to work through them. Distress and panic are most likely to grip one when feelings are allowed to remain shadowy, ominous, ghostlike shapes dancing around the edges of our conscious mind. When those wraithlike horrors can be forced to take shape, they can be dealt with.

That's the reason for talking about them. Words help give them form and shape, taking them out of the shadows of mystery into the light of conscious inspection. Unless one begins to talk out loud to oneself (an activity which is highly suspect in our society!), someone else must be willing to listen without judging.

In Southern California we have what we call "high morning fog." Mornings are cloudy until 10 or 11 o'clock when the sun becomes hot enough to burn the fog away. Talking about feelings with a warm, accepting person is like letting the heat of the sun burn away the fog that wraps them in shadowy anonymity. Feelings that have form and shape yield to analysis, diagnosis, and prayer. All the powers of the mind and spirit can focus on them; their effect on the body can be studied and understood.

A form of physical therapy known as Rolfing (after Ida Rolf who first used it) operates on the principle that emotions originating in crisis, unless expressed and dealt with at the time they are experienced, become locked in to the muscle structure. Certain emotions affect certain sets of muscles, depending on the time of life and the circumstances in which those emotions were experienced. As a skilled therapist who understands both psychology and body structure works with the patient's muscles, the patient recalls vividly as a conscious memory-picture the event which was locked in to certain muscles. Perhaps it

40

was sexual abuse or a terrible beating by a parent. But whatever caused the original pain, as it is released by the therapist's often painful manipulations, the client experiences emotional healing from that long-buried mental and physical pain sealed into the affected muscles.

Our body, mind, and spirit form an interrelated whole. Feelings cannot be denied and repressed without doing violence to every other area of our living. Monica's inability to talk about her feelings destroyed her marriage and made her physically ill. Linnie's lack of listeners almost drove her to commit murder. To keep my repressed feelings from erupting, I needed an intensely demanding schedule of busyness which produced a great deal of tension.

We commonly postpone the "moment of truth" as long as possible. We fantasize: the departed lover will return; death is not real; my employers will discover that they can't do without me and offer me my old job back again; the cancer will go away and I'll be healthy again.

The critical moment comes when the chilling reality of my abandonment overwhelms me—he really does *not* love me, I *am* alone, she *is* dead, they really *can* do without me. Cold reality numbs the spirit and casts me into a dark pit of despair.

This is the critical moment of utter aloneness, of total abandonment, the horror at the bottom. Unless we can find some stirring of strength in ourselves, or unless God moves in, there's no place to go but to suicide, alcohol, drugs, new dependencies.

Out of the horror at the bottom, I can scream and cry, but the only echo that comes back to me is, "Why live? Kill yourself! No one cares anyway."

Jesus, help me and all others experiencing that horror at the bottom! It's real, it's overwhelming, and to deny it is to keep it alive.

Something to think about

1. What were your *immediate* feelings during your critical moment?

_____ I felt like I was going to pieces.

_____ I felt like vomiting.

_____ I felt like screaming and crying.

_____ I felt icy and numb.

_____ I felt like committing suicide.

_____ I felt like I could never be forgiven.

_____ I felt like hurting someone as much as I had been hurt.

_____ I felt all alone, abandoned, forsaken.

_____ I was terribly afraid.

_____ I felt like God was with me.

On the following pages, describe as fully as you can your feelings at the time of the critical moment in your life. By writing them down, you release them. They stand apart from you. They have shape and form, and you can deal with them on a conscious level.

But don't stop reading this book after you have written them down! Go on to the end immediately to experience healing and renewal.

3

WHEN STRENGTH COMES OUT OF HIDING

Dena told me the story of her great-grandmother.

I loved to talk to Grandpa. His mother and father homesteaded in the western part of South Dakota and Peder (my grandfather) and his little sister Krista were born there. When Peder was nine years old, his father was killed by a stray bullet during a holdup in the little town where they went to trade. Peder's mother died shortly afterwards. As Grandpa used to say, "What else could she do out there on the prairie but die?" Some neighbors took the little sister, but nine-year-old Peder was left to survive as best he could, speaking nothing but Norwegian, out there on the prairie.

I was fascinated by this story, especially when I considered all of its implications. *What else was there for her to do but die?* A woman alone was not expected to survive, so she didn't, but a little boy of nine was, and did!

Most of us who are born female have lived in dependency roles much of our lives. From earliest childhood we were told that we need help—if not in so many words, then by all the actions indicating that girls were weak and needed protection. We felt good about being "daddy's little girl," and we were told so many times that girls don't play rough, climb trees, or do physically demanding things; they might get hurt.

Recently a Marine officer was talking about how well female recruits are doing in their training. "The first thing they have to learn," she said in the television interview, "is to keep on going even when the pain sets in. You know, women have always been told to stop exercising when it begins to hurt, but to make it in the Marines, women have to learn to keep on after the pain starts. And they are making it!"

You have to learn to go on even when the pain starts in order to experience strength! That means unlearning most of what we're told as girls. By the time we are adults, we have really come to believe that females are weak and need someone to take care of them. The equation reads like this: "Girls are weaker than boys. I am a girl. Boys are supposed to take care of girls. Therefore, since I am weak, I will never cope with life unless someone takes care of me."

That someone cannot be another woman or girl since all females are weak, so we believe we need a man—a father, brother, boyfriend, husband, or a male pastor, lawyer, or doctor. Could this be the reason women are frequently the most vigorous opponents of women doctors, pastors, pilots, presidents? We have learned well our cultural lessons: women are weak and incapable of the strengths which leadership demands.

The need to be taken care of is strong in all of us— male and female—but boys are told from the time they are very young that they are going to have to be strong, whether or not they feel strong, because they are the ones who are going to have to take care of the world's weak ones, namely women and children.

A majority of boys grow up accepting their highly responsible and stress-filled roles and discharge their obligations toward the demanding society quite well, especially if their wives assume a role that is highly supportive of their husbands' responsibilities.

Other boys experience a great deal of pressure trying to prove that they are strong enough to bear the burdens of the women in their lives, even though the role is contrary to their natures. Some live with ulcers and high blood pressure, until finally they break down physically and die of a sudden heart attack or other stress-related ailment. In other cases, the breakdown is emotional and they become alcoholic or desert their families.

When that happens, dependent women are left without all the male support they were taught to believe was needed if they were to survive and was their right to expect. Emotionally unprepared and with skills unequal to the demands made on them for total support, these unmarried, divorced, deserted, widowed and role-reversed women are in crisis! Their protected, sheltered existence proves to be a house of glass which shatters into a million pieces and exposes them to the chill winds of abandonment. Crisis laughs at their learned dependency.

Alone and abandoned—the critical moment! The horror at the bottom is real.

Some women just give up and die, like Peder's mother in her sod hut on the prairie. Others, like hundreds of pioneer women who did not die when they were alone in their huts or in wagon trains on the long westward trail, sense a stirring of strength in their spirits, a flutter of their wills, a flexing of psychic muscles, and a stiffening of their backbones, and they begin to march to a different drumbeat: "*I am not helpless!* Nothing can destroy me; I will survive!"

Like Scarlett O'Hara in *Gone with the Wind,* the sheltered, helpless clinging vine withers and dies and is reborn as an indomitable oak. Tiny, almost afraid to push its trembling shoot out of the ground where it lay buried, the oak begins to grow. "I will never be hungry again!" Scarlett vowed, and at that moment she realized that she alone was going to have to take responsibility for making that resolution come true. No other human could be depended upon, ever again, to do it for her.

Destroyed is the myth of feminine helplessness. All the things that women in crisis have been told they could never do because they were girls (and "girls" they would be called until they died!) suddenly need to be done. *Strength is born when they stop asking "Why?" and start asking "How?"* The *why* gets laid to rest for most of us when we begin to believe the promise that "all things work together for good to them that love God, to them who are called according to his purpose" (Rom. 8:28 KJV).

When Abby's husband deserted her, leaving her with a six-month-old daughter, no food, no clothes except the ones they were wearing, and no money for support, she was so frightened that she stopped eating and lost 25 pounds. Like Scarlett, she thought she would starve to death. Then came that strange stirring within. What was it? A strange feeling to be sure. Relief. Yes, she felt relief because "a lot of pain and a heavy burden that I hadn't even been realizing I was carrying left with him."

Then Abby became aware of another phenomenon. All those people who had rallied around and given her help (and how she had needed them those first weeks!) suddenly became a barrier protecting her from her own resources. "I almost felt guilty," she writes. "It dawned on me that I felt stronger when they weren't around. I guess when others were around I had come to depend on them to take care of me. When I was alone I depended on myself and God. And when that happened, I found a strength that I have never known before. And it was *my own strength!*"

Isn't it ridiculous to have to pretend to be weak so we won't hurt others' feelings? But what a familiar echo that triggers in the hollow chambers of our memories. "Girls shouldn't be too smart; they won't be popular. Boys especially don't like strong girls. You've got to make them feel strong by acting weak and helpless. That's more feminine!"

According to extensive research, carried on for 20 years with more than 20,000 subjects (approximately 14,000 women and 7,000 men) from the United States and many other countries quite different in culture, this perception of what women need to be to please men may be totally false. On the basis of this study using the MAFERR Inventory of Feminine Values, it appears that what women want for themselves and what men want them to be is in basic agreement, but women don't believe it. Women universally share a desire to combine self-fulfilling activities outside the home with the traditional nurturing roles, but they perceive a conflict between the independence they would like for themselves and the passivity and dependence which they think men want from them.

On the test men consistently picture their ideal woman as one who achieves a balance between family orientation and self-orientation. Essentially men want as much self-realization for women as the women want for themselves, but the women don't realize it (*Women in Thera-*

py, edited by Violet Franks and Vasanti Burtle, Brunner/Mazel, New York, pp. 54-59).

Perhaps we *want* to stay helpless and dependent and we deceive ourselves by insisting that that's the way men like us to be. Can it be a way of getting out of responsibility?

Real or fancied, in thousands of words and ways, women think they hear another social message: "Be weak, and a man will take care of you." That's why Abby almost died of starvation when her husband left. She had come to believe that she could not survive on her own as a woman alone.

> I would not be the strong person I am today living a much better life if I had not been *forced* to take care of myself. My only regret is that I didn't learn that lesson earlier! I was sheltered and dominated by my loving parents and not given the opportunity to find out my own strength. I'm conscious of this in raising my own children now. I feel it's important that they know and like themselves and can depend on themselves for the strength they need to live a productive life. I am guiding them this way and it will not take them as long as it did me to find direction in their own lives.

> If I had been a stronger person throughout my marriage my husband would probably have been a stronger man. *Weak people drag everybody into their own weakness.* I have really come to believe that.

> Maybe we had too much togetherness and never did our own thing. I think I was too possessive and clinging. I thought that was the way a wife should be. Now I realize what a drag I must have been on him all those years!

I asked a friend who is in charge of chaplaincy services for several child-care centers in California what he thought parents could do to help their children find strength to live in this fast-paced world. His answer: "Most well-intentioned parents, especially parents in the church, take too many lumps for their children. They want to protect them from pain and hurt and the kids never get a chance to develop their own strengths."

The pain Abby suffered when no one was there to take her lumps for her was so devastating that it took three years before she could love another man enough to give herself without holding back. In the meantime, during those lonely years, she had grown in her own self-esteem so that she could love him, not because she *needed* him, but because she *wanted* him.

Kim, whose husband left her with three children when she was 29, came out of a period of "hiding when I didn't want to talk to anyone—family, friends or neighbors" to discover that she didn't need to hide, waiting for some-one to give her strength. She, too, says:

> I'm sorry I wasn't more independent from the start. All of our self-worth shouldn't come from one person! Why did I take all the blame and guilt for our situation and convince myself that it was all my fault? I felt so worthless. As I started to think better of myself, other things started to fall into place also. I went out and got a job and that gave me confidence. I met a whole new group of people and began to feel that life was worth living. My own strength and ability to take care of myself surprised me!

This sense of *awareness of latent strength* is one of the surprises that comes out of hiding when women are forced to help themselves or give up entirely—and die in their little sod huts.

Giving up is always the first option that comes to de-pendent persons when cast on their own resources. When the supporting props are taken away and there's nothing and no one to lean on any more, panic voices that first option, "Give up! You'll never make it alone!"

As Amy said when her marriage of 30 years fell apart, "I felt so lost. I felt my heart was broken in half. He was *my whole life!*"

Whenever any other human becomes our whole life, we have already lost our own life and many find it a simple step to complete the job with physical suicide.

Crisis summons forth our own God-given strength if we can make it through that critical giving-up moment.

What saved Amy and Abby and the others who lived through that moment to share their stories with me is neatly summed up by Amy when she says, "I didn't let it get the best of me. I came up from the pit in which I had fallen and found out that I could survive." And another says it this way, "I found I had an inner reserve of strength to hang on to in spite of the hurt. I made up my mind that we were simply going to get along somehow."

A *conscious decision to go on,* to survive, follows awareness of strength. Or maybe it's the other way around—first the decision and then the awareness. More likely they come into being simultaneously.

Sybil made that decision to go on living while she stood on the Narrows Bridge in Washington and contemplated jumping. A great conflict had raged in her for many years. She felt weak and inadequate. To prove that she was okay, she assumed all kinds of tasks and offices.

> I had been told all my life that I was no good and I wanted to prove that I really was worth something, but it never worked. I got to the point where I felt I just couldn't go on any longer. So I stood on the bridge for a long time that day and the temptation to jump was powerful. But, trembling and ex-

hausted, I came off that bridge with the decision that I was going to live and God would help me find the strength, no matter what. I'd never find all the strength I needed in what others said about me (or didn't say about me), but if God said I was okay, then I could believe in myself and find the strength to go on.

At the critical moment, you decide how you're going to face the whole business of living. You recognize that *you actually do have a choice.* You can decide to face life with depression or without depression, with psychosomatic illness or without psychosomatic illness, with insanity or without insanity.

Who would *choose* to be depressed, or insane, or sick? Those choices aren't made on the conscious level. But every time someone asks, "How are you?" we choose how to respond. We may choose words that rehearse our sad, depressed feelings or describe our physical symptoms—be they stomach pains, cramps, diarrhea, headaches—or we may choose to talk about our feelings of disorientation and confusion. Often we give such a response because of a choice we've made somewhere in our psyche that it's better to suffer from depression or physical illness or mental aberrations than it is to suffer the pain of being helpless and inadequate and not very lovable.

In the last chapter I underlined the importance of expressing feelings honestly. And I still say that. Express your true feelings at the time of crisis—grieve, cry, be angry. Get it all out, or you will never get rid of your pain.

Depression, however, is only a symptom of other feelings. Depression has been defined as "anger turned inward." What, or whom, is the anger against? Symptoms of illness are often an outward expression of some hidden pain that is taking physical shape. That pain is usually caused by a sense of inadequacy and inability to cope with feelings of helplessness. Acting crazy is a way of getting out of a real world that produces feelings too painful to deal with in one's right mind.

So the real feelings and memories underneath all of these symptoms need to be identified and expressed. But once they've been expressed and dealt with, a decision must be made to move on, to explore options for surviving, to face the "how" of living. That decision actualizes a growing awareness of the survival strength God has built into every living creature, including women.

Those who will navigate their way safely through their critical moments are those who refuse to settle for negative responses. They *act* on their tiny stirrings of strength. They don't sit in the slime of their pit and rehearse its horrors; they begin to explore it and start carving handholds in the sides. All those excuses for giving up—"I don't have an education"; "I don't have a marketable skill"; "I haven't worked for 20 years"; "I'm just a woman"; "I'm too old"; "I'm too young"—all excuses lose their power.

A 66-year-old woman who was suddenly widowed decided that she would go back to school and learn auto mechanics so she could repair her own car. Before long she was studying real estate. But at the time of her husband's death, she says, "I didn't see how I could go on living. He did everything for me. I had never really been on my own or worked to earn my own living. I grew up believing that the husband should make all of the decisions. It's a wonder I survived at all. Just sheer determination, I guess."

She's right. The strength that's dug out by sheer determination has been there hiding all the time under that learned dependency.

Decision-making comes easier if you've had some practice before the critical moment occurs. But not many of us have had as much of that as Dody. When her husband was killed in that car racing accident, she was able to say:

> I am a realist and have learned over the years to cope with whatever hand was, or is, dealt to me. I think that's one of the reasons I have survived this crisis as well as I have so far. I've always been an organized person who can take on more than one project at a time and know which priorities come first. I think I have my head on straight. I am able to think out my situation and make decisions. I tend to be reserved but can also be outgoing when necessary; it's a combination of being both dependent and independent. I'm not really a homebody but I take seriously being a mother to my boys.

> I've always had my own interests and my husband had his interests. We shared them and could talk about them but we didn't need to be together all the time. We were both happy. If we didn't like something the other did we were able to talk it out. It was a top priority that I knew the financial situation in both our business and personal life because that's the way we both wanted it.

Dody doesn't talk about having an easy time of it, but her decision-making ability helped her weigh one option against another.

For Dolly, divorced at 24, and for Eve, whose marriage broke up when she was 42, having to make decisions was agonizing. Dolly says that she was most depressed during the decision-making period before the actual parting of the ways. During that time she felt "trapped, very insecure, unsure of what either decision would hold for me. And *frightened!* But once the decision had been made and I started immediate action to start a new life, I found release. It was to prove a growing experience, but full of pain, and now I'm a stronger person for having weathered the storm. But believe me, it wasn't easy. Just a matter of one step at a time, with each step bringing a little more strength with it."

Eve had similar feelings before the decision. But her "immediate feeling after the decision was one of *relief* along with a firm resolution to stay by that decision because it had been such a long struggle to reach that point. For me *the important thing was to make a decision* and to believe in my own ability to make the right one. If you once start to doubt yourself, you're sunk!"

Friends play an important role in helping us survive a crisis. But to become aware of our own strength and to learn to make our own survival decisions, we need time to be alone. In some cases women have felt that the constant presence of others was a hindrance to both prayer and their growing strength. As Andrea said:

> Neighbors and friends were so good to invite me to their homes, and I went visiting a great deal with my family. I would have liked to have been alone a little more after my husband was killed in the train accident, but there were people around all the time. I needed the silence, but could never get alone. I remember leaving the room where friends were gathered those first days and someone always following me. I guess they were afraid to let me be alone and maybe it was best that way, but I think I could have grown in strength a lot faster if I had gotten off by myself and found that strength in myself and my own relationship with God.

I recall having the same experience after my husband

broke his neck. For the first few weeks I never had a chance to be alone. One of my children would go with me to the hospital and sit with me in the waiting room. Apparently they had agreed that whenever I left the house one of them would go with me. They obviously feared that I might do something desperate or have a breakdown. I finally reassured them that I needed some time to be alone so I could think and pray things through, gather my own resources and tap my own inner strength. To have people available when I needed them was good, but their constant presence became a hindrance to growth.

Choosing not to be a "victim" helps strength come out of hiding. We have to face the fact that sometimes we *like* to be victims because that gets us a certain amount of attention we would not otherwise have. My mother used to call it "pulling the poor mouth." Whenever people enjoy talking about how little they have, how sick they are, and how mistreated they are, it may be out of an intuitive understanding that "underdogs" get more sympathy than people "on top." The strong have to stand alone, and sometimes it's pleasant to be weak and to be taken care of.

But how good it is to be strong when one cannot be taken care of! At that point the choice must be made not to be a victim. Self-made victims blame something else or someone else for their weakness—poor parenting, the system, cultural norms, crippling accidents or illness. But for every victim of circumstances "beyond their control," one can name others who have transcended the same circumstances, found strength to cope with them and even to do well in spite of them (or perhaps *because* of them.)

Frequently the help of an objective counselor is required to enable us to recognize the bad choices we are making and to help us examine options for good choices, but options do exist. The first step can only be taken when we decide which direction we want to move. The choice is ours.

The most significant choice may be to admit we need help. But that choice must be the result of our own decision and not what others have decided for us. To tell another person that he or she is weak and cannot get along without our help only increases the person's feelings of inadequacy and takes away his or her initiative. We deepen the person's weakness and dependency.

Sadie tells about a decisive turning point in her life. "I had lost most of the potassium in my system through taking high blood pressure medicine. I found out that I wasn't in complete control of my body functions, and it really made me realize that God is in control. So now I just let God be in control. There really is no other way as far as I'm concerned, but I had to make the choice myself to put my life in those loving hands."

A great deal of wisdom lies in not continuing to beat one's head against the proverbial brick wall. If giving in and admitting that maybe we do need help is the best choice, that's a strong decision in itself. Experience tells us that "time heals" and brings growth and strength, so a decision to be patient and wait may be best. Doesn't Isaiah tell us that "they who wait for the Lord shall renew their strength" (40:31)? Waiting is an integral part of the strengthening process.

Whenever our bodies have sustained a wound of any kind, the first thing medical people do is try to stabilize our vital signs. They couldn't operate on Erling's broken neck until they were sure his vital signs—blood pressure, pulse, respiration—were stable.

When my 82-year-old mother was visiting me she fell backwards off the front stoop on to the pavement below and sustained a deep scalp laceration. The paramedics came immediately in answer to our call. She was bleeding profusely from her scalp and my first thought was that the paramedics should bind up the wound and stop the bleeding. Instead they ignored the obvious wound and immediately took her blood pressure reading, pulse, and respiration. This gave them exact knowledge as to how her body had survived the shock of the fall. When they were satisfied that her blood pressure was all right, they tended the scalp wound.

After any trauma to the mind, body, or spirit (and whenever one is affected they are all affected), a period of stabilization is required. This simply takes time. Knowing this, we understand why it may be a sign of strength to say, "I can wait. I can be patient and not expect miracles of strength and recovery to happen at once. I'm not going to rush myself or make any fantastic leaps into a new life. I'll give myself time to adjust to the new situation and not make any other decision than to *wait* at this time."

A sense of expectancy characterizes waiting more than inactivity does. During this time of stabilization, many women find that having certain tasks to do enables their recovery. Danielle says that she found strength in "the necessity to keep going for my children's sake, plus a garden that needed care. I threw myself into digging and planting and the pain began to dull."

A sense of responsibility for children often plays a large part in motivating women to carry on, but an equally large number of women said that it was their job in the business or professional world that kept them going during their time of strength-gathering. Hazel believes she would never have survived the automobile accident that claimed the life of her only daughter if she had not been deeply involved in her work. A woman who was 65 when her crisis occurred says emphatically,

"If I had been younger I would have gone to work! I've seen it happen time and again that women who have something to do outside the home seem to get along so much better than those of us who stay home."

Many women experience fear when faced with the prospect of moving out of their houses into the workaday world. Two things seem to contribute to this fear. One is the dependency women have accepted as their natural state. The second, growing out of the first, is guilt for doing something that is against that "natural" order.

Women have come to me with anxiety and terror when they are about to go to an interview *alone* or take a plane trip *alone,* with the comment that "my father always did that for me" or "my husband always took care of that." They fear all those unknown and unlearned processes such as making plane and hotel reservations, renting cars, attending committee and board meetings where the agenda belongs to men. They seek "pink-collar" jobs which society reserves for women and which are generally in a lower wage category because it takes all the courage they can muster just to face a minimal reentry into the world outside the home.

Symbolically, women are carried over the threshold of a house in which they will live as bride, wife, and mother. When those relationships become null and void through death, divorce, or desertion, some women almost seem to need to be carried forcefully back out into the world and retrained for living outside the protective walls of a house.

Psychologists call that kind of fear "agoraphobia," fear of open places. I experienced agoraphobia when I first accepted speaking engagements around the country. Later, when I had to go to work following Erling's crippling accident, I was terrified at the thought of braving that sophisticated world beyond the walls of my home.

I hadn't been out there alone for decades! What did I know about airports, limousine service to motels, staying alone in alien hotels, eating alone in strange restaurants, finding my way around unfamiliar cities? The thought of being in locations where I didn't know anyone and could not contact a familiar person shattered me.

Can I adequately express my panic in some of these situations? But Dolly and Eve have already said it so well. Their solution was mine, too. Take one step at a time. The first time around is the toughest of all, like the first time you have to drive a strange car around unfamiliar streets in a foreign city. I recall driving an Audi (I had never been in one before) on the Autobahn (a freeway similar to the Indianapolis Speedway) from Bonn (I couldn't even pronounce it correctly) to Düsseldorf—and all the signs along the way were in German, truly a foreign language to me.

Suffice it to say, I lived to tell you about the experience. More than that, I *enjoyed* it. Nothing quite equals the sense of exhilaration that comes from trying something new, something you fear, and succeeding at it. Unless you face the fear and move into it, it will always control your life—and confine you to immobility.

I try to help myself in some ways. I often do a behavioral rehearsal before I go into a strange situation. I get into a comfortable, relaxed position, close my eyes, and imagine myself going through the steps necessary to accomplish the goal. If that goal is an interview for a new job, I think about getting ready for the interview. What will I wear? I imagine myself putting my clothes on, fixing my hair, going through all the necessary steps. I see myself doing them.

I go through every step in the same way. If I feel my fear rising, I go back to relaxing and retrace my steps until I no longer feel anxious at that step. I visualize my interviewer, try to picture the person. Woman or man? Young or old? By the time I get through I have a familiar picture of a person and we are conversing quite easily. I hear myself speaking wisely, laughing delicately, looking properly assertive and at the same time gentle and modest. I never visualize failure.

Most important of all, I visualize God's Spirit in me, giving me comfort, guidance, wisdom, freedom from fear, and power to perform well. Since I have no difficulty believing that God's Spirit dwells in me as a consequence of my faith in Jesus Christ, I can also believe that the Spirit is with me wherever I go. I see that Presence quite clearly in my mind as I relax and go through my steps to success.

Psychologists have a process called systematic desensitization similar to the one I use. It involves learning to relax and making up a hierarchy of easy-to-hard pictures of fearful situations to focus on in order to conquer a phobia. It's a helpful technique but lacks an ongoing strengthening force which can enable one to handle any phobic situation. God's Spirit provides that strengthening force through faith in Jesus Christ.

I find 2 Timothy 1:7 helpful as I move into frightening situations: "For God did not give us a spirit of timidity but a spirit of power and love and self-control." There goes my panic! I *can* control myself in strange situations. The promise of Jesus in Matthew 28:20 assures me that whenever I am on his mission, he is there: "And lo, I am with you always."

One woman set a goal of daily Bible reading and a period of unfailing prayer for her daughter, who

> had an early adolescence seasoned with tension and strife between her and us. At the time she entered high school we moved to a new city to a happier job for my husband. Our daughter "flipped out," refused

to adjust, and my husband gave her a choice—stay and follow house rules or go if you want to continue this way. She left and grief set in as if she had died. It seemed an irreparable separation. When I read about grief resulting from the death of a loved one, I could relate to that.

This woman started writing a daily journal describing her feelings of fear, guilt, and grief, but she ended each day's entry with a thought full of hope and promise. Now when she looks back on that journal, she sees how far she has come in understanding herself and her situation. She also took a course in adolescent psychology and learned how to communicate with teenagers.

She refused to be a victim and took positive steps toward growth in what otherwise was a devastating situation. Looking back, she is able to say "Thank God for this opportunity to grow." She is not demanding immediate answers to her prayers. Part of her strength lies in her willingness to wait. She knows that she needs time to grow in understanding of her daughter, and that her daughter also needs time to mature.

Survival strengths are God's creative gifts, hidden in the nature of every human being, to be used at will. I believe there are no limits to the possibilities open to any one of us, no matter what the circumstances of our lives. One of the most fascinating lecturers I've ever heard was severely crippled by polio. People with incurable cancer often give strength to all of the "well" people around them.

And you may have read about Joni Eareckson, the courageous young woman who was paralyzed from the shoulders down by a diving accident when she was 17. Initially she was plunged into despair, but today she draws beautiful pictures with pencils held in her teeth, and her good cheer and indomitable faith uplift everyone she meets.

Such people do not waste their precious energies on self-pity and demeaning self-criticism. Instead they accept themselves as they are and move on from that point. Nothing will destroy us faster than constant self-criticism.

A few summary statements are in order:

1. Stop asking "why" and move on to "how."

2. Take charge of your own survival and make your own choices, moving head on into your fears.

3. Decide for yourself what help you need; don't be a victim.

4. Be willing to wait, allowing time for mind, body, and spirit to recover.

5. Trust that all things are working together for good, even though you cannot see it now. Joy *will* come.

6. Find tasks to do which keep your hands busy during the waiting.

7. Trust God's indwelling Spirit working through your own brain to open doors to a new life beyond crisis.

One of the gifts of crisis is the discovery of your own inner strength.

Something to think about

What helped you to get beyond "why" to "how"? Describe it on the next page.

List on this page the strengths you have discovered in yourself as a result of your crisis.

4

WHEN GOD MOVES IN

The border between the United States and Mexico is guarded by a strong chain-link fence with rolls of loosely coiled barbed wire along the top. Bare open ground 100 yards wide along the fence offers no hiding place for those who want to cross the border illegally. Guards patrol the territory day and night. Yet thousands of people cross that border without permission every year.

One of the startling discoveries in crisis is that *strong is never strong enough!*

Carrie found that out when she was at what she thought was the peak of her strength. She had survived many crises in her 27 years—illness, a crippling accident to her father, several moves to new locations during her adolescent years, a broken romance—and her worst crisis came when she had attained a long-awaited goal, a moment of triumphant victory over great odds. After many years of starting and stopping to cope with various crises, she had finally finished college. She felt strong and victorious and ready to live.

That doesn't sound like the prelude to a crisis, but for her it was. Everything might have gone along fairly well after graduation except that eight months later she still had not found a job. Graduation with honors, great references—and no one hired her! Carrie sent her story to me.

I signed up with several employment agencies; I had friends looking for jobs for me; I went on interview after interview. One after another they proved fruitless. Either I didn't have enough experience or they wanted me to start at a job that paid so little that there was no way I ever could support myself. Gradually my high spirits drooped as I came home from interviews tired and discouraged to spend the night crying and pleading for God's guidance and help.

At the same time I felt that God had given up on me. I had survived many obstacles, grown so strong, and accomplished so much—but none of it was doing me any good. I began to doubt God's existence. It was all an illusion, I thought. I prayed for death, convinced that I didn't want to go on living. Nothing excited me, not visiting anyone, not going anywhere. I withdrew from all my friends and found myself fearful to even leave the house. The strength I thought I had was a mirage. I was as weak and dependent as ever. If I ventured out to do some shopping I panicked, fearful that I was going to faint or scream or go crazy before I got back home. I had visions of being hauled off to a mental institution.

I began to be physically sick. I spent my 28th birthday in bed with a migraine headache. I felt like I might have a case of the flu and for two weeks I was in and out of bed, listless and without energy. All I wanted to do was sleep. (Was I looking for an excuse to get out of making interviews?) After two weeks, I still had no energy. At my doctor's suggestion, I took the glucose tolerance test for hypoglycemia and an iodine test for low thyroid. I really wasn't hypoglycemic, but "borderline," the doctor said.

That was all I needed to make me read everything I could find on the subject. I immersed myself in books on low blood sugar and convinced myself that I had all the symptoms—depression, crying, no energy, irritability, dizziness, and antisocial behavior! Now I had an excuse for acting the way I did, and certainly no one in my condition could be expected to make interviews!

A week later I experienced severe stomach and intestinal distress—distended stomach, constant gas pains, endless diarrhea. So I went back to the hospital for all of the gastrointestinal tests, including blood tests, stool cultures, barium enema, X rays. All were negative.

Thinking positive thoughts or concentrating on the Bible was impossible. I ridiculed my parents and their Christian friends as being religious frauds and I wallowed in a groove of total depression, loneliness, and aloneness. Whenever I thought about anyone, especially the people who said they were praying for me, my mind was consumed by hateful thoughts. After a time I was no longer civil to those around me. My whole personality changed. I wanted to be left alone and I was left alone (all the while longing for someone to reach out to me!)

My best friend had moved 1500 miles away some time before and, in desperation, because I couldn't communicate with people near me, I wrote to her and shared my feelings with her. I said, "I've never felt feelings like this before. Sure, I was depressed in school when I worried about grades, afraid that I might not get all A's. This is different. I'm questioning my whole life, wishing I'd never been born, wondering why God even created me. But even while I'm thinking these things, I'm afraid God will repay my doubts with some horrible disease like cancer.

"The more other people talk about their crises and what God has done in their life, the more I doubt God's love for me. I'm in such deep despair that I don't even think a miracle could get me out of it. I find the number of people I can relate to becoming fewer and fewer. I really can't stand the thought of living any longer. Everything ends up in aloneness and loneliness. That's the way it is, and the terrible thing is that no one can take care of you but yourself! And now all the strength I've built up just isn't enough!

"While I find it extremely difficult to live any longer, at the same time I know I could not take my life. What a dilemma! I'm surrounded by caring friends and family, but I feel completely alone. I can find no relief!"

At this point Carrie made what was ultimately to be a saving discovery—our own strength is never strong enough to prevent God's archenemy, the devil, from penetrating it. Like the barbed wire fence along the Mexican border, it can be crossed, penetrated, cut, crushed, mocked.

Our own strength becomes a deceiver if it betrays us into believing that we can get along without God. The strength that enables us to shrug off our human dependencies boomerangs if it makes us think we're independent of God's strength, too. We sometimes make the mistake of thinking that human strength can face tests which only God can pass.

Christ, the God/Man, passed his wilderness temptation test so we could forever after call on him to best the forces of evil on our behalf. He has *in every respect* "been tempted as we are, yet without sin. Let us then with confidence draw near to the throne of grace, that we may receive mercy and find grace to help in time of need (Heb. 4:15-16)."

The marvelous plus that nestles like a luminescent pearl at the heart of crisis is the God who moves in with healing power and comfort beyond understanding. And it's all a gift of grace! No matter how hard we fight to avoid God, to keep our lives from being invaded by the Spirit, the possibility of being surprised by the Presence is always there. Carrie tells how it happened to her.

> The day after Easter Sunday there was a transformation and I really can't explain what happened. I went to church the day before alone, avoiding people I knew, refusing to go to a family dinner gathering afterwards.

> I think on Easter Sunday I made some kind of half-hearted commitment to live—a commitment to life instead of death, with the understanding that this was *my* choice and it had nothing to do with my parents or friends or anyone else. Easter was for *me*, my own personal Resurrection Day.

> The day after Easter all of my intestinal troubles stopped and I began to feel better, like I was alive again—physically, emotionally, mentally. I had a job interview that morning *and got the job*—a job which offered a better salary than any I had previously been offered! By the next day I had received additional calls for job interviews. After months of searching and weeks of doing nothing, the speed with which I had obtained the position and the number of other calls could not have been coincidental.

> I am convinced that God was guiding my life all the time, waiting for an opportunity to get through my defenses. Right now I feel peaceful and relaxed.

I'm living minute by minute, enjoying one day at a time, knowing that Jesus Christ has already raised me from the dead!

Carrie has been resurrected. My heart is filled with love for others, feelings I thought I would never know again. The Lord is real in my life. It was a hellish experience arriving at this point but now I know that the agony was worth it. I'm thankful for an opportunity to express this miracle in my life! Praise be to God!

Though for her it was unique, Carrie's experience has its counterpart in the experience of others. But the thought that such renewal is common does not comfort anyone currently struggling with a God-crisis. Philosophers have and are wrestling with questions of What is reality? What is truth? What is good? At the heart of them all is the final question, Is there a God out there, and if there is, what does that have to do with me?

Discovery of personal strength is one of the beautiful things to come out of crisis, but discovery of God as the inexhaustible source of that strength is the ultimate good. Even the strongest person, the most well-integrated personality, the one with all the resources of wealth and education and family and friends, finds all of it worthless if there is no ultimate answer to "Why am I here? What am I living for?"

The discovery that "God is *real* and *real for me*" is the miracle of a God who moves in, surprising us with joy in the middle of pain, comfort in our lonely abandonment, and power in place of our phobias and fears.

Lou had gone along as a casual Christian in a rather formalistic church until the night she went with a friend to another church where she witnessed an exorcism in which a girl was "delivered from demon possession."

Lou was plunged into an occult world of darkness and fear which almost destroyed her.

> I would like to give this as my testimony to anyone else who may be tormented by the kind of fear I had after seeing that young woman convulsing in the grip of a power that was almost visible in the room.

> Fear so took hold of me that I nearly suffered a nervous breakdown. The experience lasted for weeks. At its worst I could not sleep. I could only hold on to my sanity for dear life. I wanted to escape, to go back to where I had been before—casual, nonchalant, taking my religion for granted. You see I had not known that kind of spiritual world and it frightened me. I was exposed to another power that I had not accepted as real before.

> I was not really delivered until the night when I faced the worst of my fears (that I was going to lose my mind), and accepted the possibility that it might happen and that I would still trust the Lord. I literally said to God, "All right, if following you and living in your kingdom means that I will lose my mind, then I'll lose it, but no matter what, I'm sticking with you."

> It took weeks of suffering to bring me to that place, but I finally laid down my life and I surrendered to God. Recovery was not instant, but I am whole and solidly founded on the Rock. I am full of joy and peace and I bless the Lord. I'm so free to share God's love with others now. Though I suffered more than I had ever suffered before, through it I have learned to depend on God and not on my own strength. The Lord has opened doors of ministry that would never have been possible without that suffering.

> So I praise God for it because fear ruled me and made me recognize my weakness. I made a choice

on faith that required me to give all or nothing of my life to Christ.

Crises are not a series of isolated events, but they are part of an ongoing process of change and growth. Carrie and Lou were Christians before, but crisis marked the transition from one stage of awareness to another. Being set free from sin, death, and the power of the devil is a daily need and a daily possibility. In the process doors are opened into painful and frightening areas of one's spirit, but doors also open to new experiences of God's power and to new ways of behaving which increase their effectiveness as Christian witnesses.

Carrie had lived her life in a rigid way, scheduling everything she did—washing her hair every morning at a certain time and in a certain way, even weighing out her food to stay on her rigidly prescribed, self-imposed diet. If anyone interrupted her schedule, she sometimes was extremely irritated. Her crisis forced her to see that she could not always control her body or emotions or other people, and she is now much more likable, relaxed, and less controlling.

Lou had been intolerant of people with other religious experiences and quite comfortable and shallow in her own, but her crisis forced her to accept people with radically different religious practices and to enlarge her perceptions of that invisible world where powers outside of human experience wage war with one another.

These women are now experiencing new richness in their faith and relationship with the Lord. The breakthrough came when they decided to let go of the burden which no human strength can support, to give in, to accept God's presence and strength as real for them.

For Rose that understanding came when she learned that her only daughter's marriage was breaking up after less than one year.

74

It was as though God was turning his face away from me. I had the strange urge to draw all the curtains and drapes and later realized that it meant that I wanted to shut out the world. I didn't need anyone, I thought. I wanted nothing to do with God or people, but after several months I cried out to God to take my burden. I wanted no more of it. The weight was lifted and I received peace. It was a complete peace and it led me to a deeper and trusting faith. If I could do it over again, I would relinquish the problem to God sooner. I was trying to carry it all alone in my own strength, blaming myself for having failed my daughter. But thanks be to God who gives us the victory through our Lord Jesus Christ!

Occasionally women recalled instances of "psychic" phenomena which I believe are part of the Spirit's ministry during crisis, the way God breaks through to us when there is no other way to reach us. Lori and her husband were on a four-day vacation in a neighboring state, their first in 11 years. Their son Ken had been home two months after three years of army duty. He had begun a steady job just that week. He was the only one at home, since his sisters were all married, and he was the only one who knew his parents' whereabouts.

But a card sent by Lori to one of their daughters led the State Patrol to them as they traveled on the road 300 miles from home. The officer told them about their son's death.

Ken was driving alone around narrow curves on a two-lane road to a viewpoint on the Columbia River, to see it for the first time since returning from overseas. A truck swerved and knocked his car off the cliff. But the strangest thing had happened the night before. My husband and I were awakened simultaneously. We both jumped out of bed and ran to the door of our motel room. There was no one there, so we looked at each other and said in the same breath, "Why are we awake?" There was no feeling of panic or fear, but just a strange sense of peace which we shared with each other. We went back to bed and to sleep. The clock said 1:35 a.m. So did Ken's death certificate.

Connie, a college professor, knew that her friend had died *before* word came.

When I arrived at my desk Friday morning, there was a note regarding Doris' death. It came as no surprise to me; I already knew it. That morning I dreamed that we were having a meeting of our staff in the president's office. It was very dark in there— so dark that I could not recognize the stranger sitting on the couch with two other staff members. When we left the room to go through the secretary's office, I saw that the stranger with the hidden face was Doris. Knowing that she was not expected to live too much longer, I wanted to tell her what she had meant to me through the years. Sensing that I had difficulty speaking, she placed her hand on my shoulder. Just then the telephone rang and I was awakened from my dream. Someone was calling to announce a change in plans. I knew that Doris had died and that there would be a message. It was confirmed when I arrived at the office.

God moves in to cushion the coming blows. Peace is frequently a gift of grace that comes beforehand to prepare the believer for what is to come. Dreams are one important vehicle for these glimpses of the future and for understanding the present.

The Bible provides much dream material as evidence

of ways God uses dreams to move into our lives. When we are awake and busy, so many obstacles prevent the Spirit of God from breaking through. Conscious resistance to things we don't want to understand or face blocks the wisdom of God from helping us work out our dilemmas.

In that period between deep sleep and wakefulness, before our conscious barriers are up and alert, God can speak through the deeper recesses of our psyche. While we often dream in symbols which are difficult to interpret with complete accuracy, dreams frequently convey solutions to our problems. Certainly Lori and Connie received messages when sleeping to which they would probably not have been sensitive during their waking hours.

During crisis periods dreams are especially significant. Imagine the tormenting crisis in which Joseph found himself when Mary told him about her pregnancy! Awake, he must have had conscious barriers to the solution God gave him. The law told him to divorce Mary and let her be stoned for adultery. His friends must have given him pious reasons why his anger was justified. Wasn't he a "good" man? And what was she compared to him?

God appeared to Joseph in a dream. The advice was simple and direct. "Do not fear to take Mary your wife."

But in the case of the Old Testament Joseph, the dream of seven fat and seven thin cows was symbolic and had to be interpreted. Most of our dreams are this kind. At one time during her crisis Carrie dreamed about herself.

> I dreamt that I was cutting myself into little pieces and at the same time trying to sew myself together. I was all alone in a big room and there was nothing there that I could use for cutting or sewing, but still

it was happening. I must have been cutting myself apart with my own hand, like I was my own weapon against myself. And I had no feeling about being cut, but I was just frantic with the desire to sew myself together again. I was working so hard at that when I woke up. The dream was very vivid. I recalled the horror of seeing myself all in those little pieces, but most of all I had this terrifying desire to be put together again.

Carrie interpreted her own dream as a hopeful sign for herself. Who's to deny it? Carrie can best interpret her own dreams. They came from her own psyche. Though God was not distinctly present in the dream, Carrie believed she had been given a message of hope.

Sometimes dreams are a way of helping us deal with our fears. Our daughter Kristi, who was in the ocean with her father when he broke his neck and was responsible for saving him, had nightmares for months afterwards. In her dream she rescued her father from the wave on which he was floating, only to have another wave come and snatch him away. She hunted in vain for his body and would waken screaming and crying because she had lost him, only to experience relief when wakefulness brought realization that he had not been lost in the ocean. Through her dreams, her subconscious prevented her from pushing her feelings down where she could not deal with them.

The language of dreams puzzles us with its symbolism. Danger comes when others try to interpret our dreams for us. As in Carrie's case, our dreams belong to us. All of the actors in my dreams represent some part of me. Even the objects in my dream are a projection of me.

When Lila was being divorced from her second husband, she dreamt that a toilet stood right in the middle of her living room. It was full of feces and when she tried to flush it, it wouldn't drain. Instead it kept on flushing, whirling the vile stuff in it around and spattering it on the walls and ceiling of her living room. She was in a frenzy to stop the toilet from messing up the room and she ran around trying to wipe the mess off the walls. Wherever she wiped, she only made it worse, creating smears of fecal matter and urine.

In the middle of her despair and frenzy, a man in a clean white suit appeared. The toilet stopped flushing and the walls suddenly were clean. With a sense of humor, Lila told me that she thought she had "Mr. Clean" of the television ads all mixed up with Jesus Christ and his white robes. But under the humor was a trembling flame of hope that the mess in her life could be cleansed by God's grace in Christ. This was her interpretation of the dream: "I am that living room and the toilet and its mess are inside of me. I see that as sin and it's fouled up my whole life. No matter how hard I try to clean myself up, and how I've tried, I just seem to mess things up more. Now I'm just going to turn the whole thing over to Jesus and let him make me clean."

Praise God for the strength you have uncovered in yourself in your crisis, but praise God that your strength isn't all there is. God moves in with grace unending to shape your strength to fit your particular crisis, and fill all the empty places in your life.

Something to think about

Do you identify with Carrie or Lou in their experience of God's invasion into their crisis moment? Why? Write on the next page.

In what ways were you surprised by God's presence? List them below.

On the next page describe a dream in which you felt that God was speaking to you.

The Dream Through Which God Invaded My Life

5

THE
CIRCLE
OF
LOVERS

When Monica was going through her lonely struggle with mental illness and had come to the place where "all I could say over and over was 'Please protect me or I will kill myself,' my doctor heard me. The next morning my friend fell into my arms crying, 'Don't ever do that, please!' I could feel her love and knew her prayers were just for me. Whenever the thought of suicide came again, I remembered her crying and her love and it kept me from acting on the thought."

Friends are a key to surviving crisis. When the tides of feeling rush in and out, crushing despair, deepening depression, shame and humiliation pummel the spirit and threaten to overwhelm one. At such a time friends are God in the flesh to the woman in crisis.

A story is told of a child who asked Mother to leave the light on in the bedroom at bedtime because "I'm afraid to be alone in the dark." Mother said, "You're not alone, you know. Jesus is with you." The child answered, "I know Jesus is with me, but I want someone with skin on."

The need for someone with skin on to touch and be touched by roots itself in our basic nature. Babies soon die if they aren't held close to a nurturing person's body for most of their infant lives. The skin is the largest of our sensory organs and the one through which we receive most of our early impressions of love and caring. Long before we can *see* love in another's eyes or hear it in the words "I love you," our skin has picked up the message through cuddling and stroking.

So God is made flesh in loving friends at the time of crisis. A touch is as meaningful as words; a look of compassion and love can speak volumes of comfort.

The clearest piece of data to emerge from both the oral and written stories shared with me came in answer to the question What helped you to survive the darkest moments of your crisis?

The choice of answers I gave as items to be checked on the questionnaire included the following: prayer, Bible study, going to church, sleeping pills, tranquilizers, alcohol, husband, pastor, and friends. *Overwhelmingly, respondents said that the greatest help in surviving came from friends.* (Sometimes those friends were also identified as family members.)

Ninety-two percent list friends first, often with exclamation points following. *Prayer* was checked by 63 percent; *pastors, counselors,* and *psychiatrists,* 36 percent; *going to church,* 31 percent; *husbands,* 29 percent (this percentage is low because in many cases the husband was a source of the crisis, as in divorce, death, or inability to communicate); *Bible study,* 15 percent; *tranquilizers and sleeping pills,* 10 percent. (The percentages do not add up to 100 because women checked as many items as they wanted to.)

No one checked alcohol, even though we know that generally throughout society women in their midyears are becoming increasingly heavy users of alcohol, especially following a "trigger event"—a crisis. If church women are finding release from pain in alcohol, they are not likely to go to weekend retreats where alcohol is not available. In that case they were not around to fill out my questionnaires.

If the congregation has anything special to offer people in pain beyond its Word and Sacrament ministry, it's a circle of "lovers." Jesus identified love as the hallmark of the Christian fellowship. He told the apostles that everyone would know they were his disciples "if you have love for one another" (John 13:35). If love isn't present in the church community, it cannot be called Christian. Jesus wasn't expressing a wistful hope; he *commanded* us to love. "A new commandment I give to you, that you love one another; even as I have loved you, that you also love one another" (John 13:34).

For Lily, whose 15-year-old daughter died in a car-truck accident, the ministry of friendship came through a younger daughter. The girl seemed to sense that her sister's room was something her mother could not face, so one day she took the bed apart and she and her friend painted the room bright orange. Lily writes:

> The carpet is bright and multicolored. It's going to help me in the morning and the evening, the times when I used to go in there and wake my darling up or tuck her in. The room is across from ours and one day when I went into it after Shirley Ann died, it didn't feel good any more. The orange paint that her sister put in there helped me realize that it was a new room for a new life. The brightness of the

colors reminded me of the brightness of the resurrection. I'm glad our daughter got the project started. I couldn't have done it alone, but now I can say, "Lord, she's better off with you. I don't want her to come back to this world. She's in a brighter place."

Sometimes women in crisis are helped by people on the job. Those people represent that day-by-day, real-world contact that's so important for keeping us in touch with the realities of life. Friends are a lifeline, wherever we find them. A woman sums it up by saying, "God gave me just the right people—beautiful people both in and out of my church and a lawyer who helped so much with all of the messy details."

Groups often provide more support than do individuals. Jesus promised that he would be present where "two or three" are gathered together. The Holy Spirit came when believers were gathered together "in one place." The gifts of the Spirit are given to individuals "for the common good." In groups those gifts are set free to build up the community, and individuals in that community find what is needed for their particular growth.

Small groups of women gathered together for the specific purpose of talking about what it means to be a woman in today's world are a phenomenon of the '60s and '70s. Groups may take the shape of traditional prayer and Bible study circles or they may be consciousness-raising groups organized around women's issues. Sometimes they are established by formal women's organizations (religious, civic, or political), or they may spring up through informal, word-of-mouth networks. Meetings are held as often as once a week in church buildings, homes, university women's centers, club rooms, or neighborhood recreational centers.

The more diverse the group is—including single and married women of every age, race, and class, with a variety of work experience—the more it serves to increase awareness of problems common to all women, and indeed to all humans. A sense of oneness, of "sisterhood," develops, which encourages open sharing. Women begin to see that they are not odd, mentally ill, or in need of therapy simply because they are experiencing strange new emotions. The exploration and development of latent abilities and long-buried ambitions is encouraged and every small step toward the goal of self-actualization is applauded. Members experience an increasing sense of worth, which is so important to recovery from the shattering blows which personal crisis and cultural discrimination have dealt to their self-esteem.

Whatever the group's origin, composition, or place of meeting, its success in providing support lies in an emphasis on the following norms:

- There is no leader.
- No one dominates the group or competes for speaking time.
- Members agree that the group is important and contract with each other to attend every meeting and to arrive on time.
- Members are allowed to speak freely without being criticized or judged by the others.
- Members' feelings, different life-styles, and backgrounds are respected and tolerated.
- Members are supportive of each other but do not offer advice.

The woman who is fortunate enough to be affiliated with such a group will survive any crisis. She will never feel alone, abandoned, and forsaken.

I have come to believe that God gives some people a special ministry of friendship. For some this becomes a professional, specialized form of friendship as it is carried on by pastors and psychologists. While some counseling theories deny the need for any special relationship between the counselor and the client, my conviction is that most effective therapy occurs when there is an empathetic understanding between the two persons.

God's Spirit creates that special sensitivity in some individuals which makes them channels of grace in the healing of others. They possess the healing gift of friendship.

A young woman named Chris prayed for the gift of friendship and found herself immersed in a crisis experience.

Before we moved here I told my husband that I had two prayers: (1) that at our next church I would find at least one person who loved life, was enthusiastic, and could be my friend. I was tired of being a loner pastor's wife. (2) I wanted to learn to be a more nurturing person.

After meeting Anita on my first visit to the new church, I told Bill, "This is it. She's the one who's going to be my friend." It was obvious to me after our first meeting that she had that spark and we could bounce our enthusiasms off each other. And I knew from observing her that she modeled some of those nurturing and uncritical characteristics that I needed so badly. I wasn't in any big rush to develop this friendship since I figured it would fall into place spontaneously when it was ready. Seven months later it happened. After a big meeting, I went up to give her a hug and put all of my love into it.

That was the beginning of a friendship unlike anything I'd ever known. We had a couple of weeks of joy, being together, getting to know one another, doing fun things, and I enjoyed listening to her chatter. Then without warning I kept waking up in the

> night and God seemed to be talking to me. I didn't
> believe it at first. I'm just not that type, I thought.
> God talked to people in the Bible—but to me? How
> ridiculous!
>
> Then I started questioning God. The message I got
> back was always the same, just as I was waking up,
> sort of half-asleep, four instructions that centered
> around my friendship with Anita, always the same
> and in the same order: 1) to *be* with her, 2) to *stay
> in the now* with her, 3) to *learn* from her, 4) to *carry
> on*, or continue with her.

Dreams again! So many times were dreams mentioned
as part of the crisis experience that I have been changed
from a skeptic of sorts to a believer in the importance
of dreams as avenues through which God comes, not
only with messages of hope and understanding, as mentioned in the previous chapter, but also with instruction
and visionary insight. These visions are likely to occur in
that borderland between sleep and wakefulness and are
difficult to distinguish as belonging to either state of
reality.

The instructions to Chris definitely came from a level
of her psychic life where dreaming alternates with con-
ceptual activity. The end product was direction and
guidance. Sometimes this is called religious intuition. I
have become convinced that it originates in the indwelling Holy Spirit's ministry to the believer. Chris was
skeptical about God speaking to individuals today. This
blocked her from being sensitive to her friend's deepest
needs. In the more receptive state between sleep and
waking, with conscious barriers more vulnerable to spiritual perceptions, those needs were recognized intuitively
and given shape in her thoughts.

The messages came for several nights in a row to over-
come her rational objections to her "visions." Most of us

have come to fear visions as a sign of mental illness, but the true visionary experience differs greatly from hallucinations in mental illness. The mentally ill cannot distinguish hallucination from reality. The person with a visionary experience knows what is real and what is a dream or a "waking" vision, and does not act inappropriately as a result. (For greater understanding of the significance of dreams, read *God, Dreams, and Revelation* by Morton T. Kelsey, Augsburg Publishing House, Minneapolis.)

When Chris asked for a ministry of friendship, she was given exactly that, but her response to her "dream" instructions was anything but positive.

> Well, I just sort of laughed and told God to "bug off," like Bill Cosby's Noah record. Each night it was more and more and I said "no and no!" I couldn't sleep; I felt like Jonah running and I couldn't hide my mind. Out of desperation from tiredness, I said, "Okay, Lord, anything you say, just let me sleep."

> It was the finality of the four instructions, especially that last one, that brought fear to me. But I decided that it didn't necessarily mean that there was anything final for her—God's timeline is not mine. It could have meant one day or one month or two years, ten years, or the rest of my life.

> On the morning I said "Yes," I learned that Anita went to the doctor for an examination and found out that she had to go to the hospital for tests. My spirit went THUD!

> Now I was really scared. "God," I said, "you know me. You know that I give my all to people—my family, everybody—and now you're asking me to get totally involved with someone who's only been a friend for a couple of weeks? What if she has a terminal

illness? But you wouldn't do that, would you, God? She was my answer to my prayer for a friend, wasn't she?"

Our friendship became a series of small crises that were separate facets of the great big one that was to change my whole life so that I would never be the same again. The compelling quality of my friendship with Anita was something I had never experienced before. My life was gradually becoming completely identified with hers as though God had set me apart, consecrating me for a special ministry to her.

Rollo May, the Christian psychologist, made the concept of "empathy" popular. Empathy, he says, is that "deeper state of identification of personalities in which one person so feels himself into the other as temporarily to lose his own identity. It is in this profound and somewhat mysterious process of empathy that . . . significant relations between persons take place" (*Art of Counseling*, p. 75). Rollo May perceived a definite link of empathy with mental telepathy, which is a transfer of ideas between persons by means beyond our known senses. This participation of personalities in each other would seem to be rather rare since it implies a complete surrendering of oneself to the empathetic situation.

How many of us are willing to go that far in our friendships? Yet that apparently is what the Spirit of God called Chris to become—a friend who was to so feel herself "into" Anita as to temporarily lose her own identity. No wonder Chris experienced fear! Only the power of love was to keep her in that God-created relationship with her friend. Not many days after her surrender to God's call to this unusual friendship, Chris found out why she had received those sleep-born instructions.

I watched her during the weeks to come, knowing she was scared about the results of her tests, full of fear, anxiety and apprehension; seeing it in her eyes and feeling it when I hugged her, watching a tear roll down her cheek and then having to promise not to tell anyone what I knew. I would go to church and meetings and watch her sparkle and be enthusiastic with everyone, listening, loving, and know that she was hurting more than they would know for a long time.

But they couldn't tell; she never let on. I prayed and prayed and was miserable. During a communion service I felt quite desperate about her and at the altar rail an idea "floated in." I prayed, "God, if all her friends knew, they would be praying for her and be concerned about her. *I'll* pray the prayers that all these people would pray if they knew. Give *me* the strength!"

I felt like I was so filled up with strength and love that I was right on the ceiling of that large church! Anita went to the hospital for another week of tests, then an operation and more weeks of tests. I began to feel all of her mental suffering, fear, anxiety, hopelessness, questions. Mostly at night, but also some in the daytime.

I was troubled by it all because it was all so new to me. How could someone who had been healthy all her life, who had never had one operation, actually feel the pain of another person's suffering? I dreamed that we were in a well together. I would be hanging by my hands from the edge while she hung from my shoulders or waist or ankles. Christ was at the top with hand outstretched, but in order to grab his hand, I would have to let go of the edge with one hand. . . . I fought the battle every night.

I made a wooden cross and wore it while she was in the hospital, even at night. When she came home, I gave it to her and made another for myself. After that there were some nights when I couldn't sleep and paced the floor in great pain. I was worried about my inability to sleep and became nervous about it, until one day she told me that at times when the nights were the worst she took the cross to bed with her and it relieved her pain! Of course. That was the pain I felt.

Out of it all, I was growing and changing. Anita read her Bible every day; I never had. In order not to be outdone and also because I needed strength with this "friendship," I started to read daily. That was exciting! I went from a couple of verses to a chapter to a whole book at a time! The Word spoke to me in more wonderful ways than I had ever known before.

Most exciting of all, as I was singing with my guitar one day, a melody and some words floated into my head to match the chords I strummed. I wrote the words down and realized that the song put her life's goals and mine together.

The song was about Christ fearing death and his friends sleeping through that time of fear. I thought of my friend facing and fearing a death from cancer and her many friends sleeping through her nights of suffering. And I was wondering, "How do I tell you that I think you are dying and I know a little of how you are feeling?" So I played my "Gethsemane Prayer" for her the day she told me, "I *know* I am healed!" I sang it for her once, and we both knew, without any more words, that she was *not* healed. More aching in my already breaking heart.

And the nurturing part of me that I had lacked all of my previous life grew and became strong, not only for Anita but for others too. I remember my prayer shortly before she died: "God, is her suffering because of me and what I can learn? If so, release us both, because I think I'm strong enough to carry on.

I can't take much more of her suffering and neither can she."

The next day I called in sick and drove to the hospital in Hollywood. She wasn't in her room so I asked at the desk. "Oh," said the woman at the desk, "she expired in the night." Expired? She—and I—were free at last.

In a daze I walked to the parking lot and sat in my car for a long time. On a small bit of paper I wrote:

> I watched you get weaker
> I felt myself get stronger
>
> I watched myself dying
> You watched yourself living
>
> Sometimes I couldn't separate the two
> I don't think you could either.
>
> It scared us both;
> I'm still frightened.
>
> Who am I?
>
> A part of me died;
> A part of her lives.

Friendship is a gift for ministry. Chris and Anita shared a friendship unusual in its dimensions. Friends enter into each other's pain as well as their joy. Jesus said, "I have called you friends, for all that I have heard from my Father I have made known to you." In friendship there is a "knowing all about you" quality which exists in no other relationship.

Chris asks, "Who am I? A part of me died; a part of her lives." And Jesus said that there is no greater love than to lay down one's life for a friend. To be a friend, part of one's life must be given to the other.

In crisis, that kind of friendship is salvation, a measure of the ultimate salvation we know in the friendship of Jesus Christ.

Something to think about

What helped you to survive *your* crisis?

___ Prayer   ___ Bible study   ___ Going to church

___ Sleeping pills ___ Tranquilizers ___ Alcohol

___ Husband   ___ Pastor   ___ Friends

Besides the things I checked, I was helped by:

If you have ever had a friendship like the one Chris and Anita shared, write about it here. Use the form of a letter to that friend.

6

THE PAIN THAT WILL NOT DIE

How many years does it take to get over the pain? Some say it never happens. "I'm working on it. . . ." Pain remains as a counterpoint to the rest of life, even though time mutes its sharpness.

At a college concert I listened to the young oboe soloist breathe a haunting refrain through the reed of her instrument. Its thin strain found its way into some tiny corner of my past and the memory wet my cheeks with its tears. I was crying for a little brother who died when I was 10 years old. So many years of other pains and joys had washed over that event, smoothing the sharp edges of recall, but the oboist had found with her plaintive wail the particular pain which belonged only to that memory.

Although the critical moment is fleeting, the wound it inflicts may require years of healing before the pain subsides.

Maggie, who divorced her alcoholic husband of 25 years, says that every minute of the three years since has been "anguish." Her situation vividly underscores a basic prescription for the healing of pain—*the need to forgive oneself.*

Although Maggie feels she could not have done differently, she is haunted by the fact that shortly after the divorce a cancer operation removed almost all of her husband's tongue and lower jawbone. "The change in his handsome face" breaks her heart, and she wonders if the emotional upheaval caused by her rejection of him may have triggered the cancer. "I couldn't forgive myself, and even now when I come home from work to an empty house to sit down and eat by myself, it's so painful that my heart actually hurts."

So many "Maggies" know all about the forgiving love of God in Jesus Christ, but they are unable to believe that this forgiveness is *for them.* The Scripture promise that the blood of Jesus Christ cleanses us from all sin (1 John 1:9) just doesn't seem adequate for their particular wrongdoing.

Maggie is beginning to have insight into herself when she says:

> God is revealing to me that my real problem is that I love to play the game of "poor little old me," and underneath it all I'm really blaming God for what happened. Why me, Lord? I'm claiming Romans 8:28 now. Although it took me over a year to even want to listen to the idea that "all things work together for good to them that love God, to them who are called according to his purpose," I'm able now to praise God for what has happened and keep thanking him for putting the pieces of my life together again—in his way and in his time. I can see that I'm not ready for reconciliation with my husband. Out of my own sense of guilt I would have

taken away his independence by waiting on him too much. For some people being forgiven may happen in an instant. But for me it's been a long and growing process. In the meantime the pain still comes.

Guilt feelings are more likely when the crisis results from one's own decision or neglect or influence, as Katie experienced when her daughter almost died from swallowing medicine left within her reach. So guilt is much more likely to develop in those cases in which women *choose* to be divorced, rather than when the husband decides.

But even when the husband initiates the divorce, women often torture themselves with such questions as What did I do to make him reject me? Was it my fault? If I had acted in a different way, would it not have happened?

Even though the actions of the husband may have provoked the divorce, as in Maggie's case, women still tend to blame themselves for the failure of the marriage. Of course we know that an individual's inability to control his or her drinking is the combination of many factors and that relationships do influence the course of alcoholism, but a woman's *incessant* self-blame probably indicates the need to remain a victim.

So while Eve, too, does not regret her decision to divorce, she says:

I would not want to ever experience those years again. I wish I could have done things differently, perhaps have confronted my husband sooner and more forcefully. I was too willing to let life take its course, so I rode it out too long. The problems became so complex until the deterioration of our marriage was inescapable. And I do so wish that I could get over my guilt about the results of our divorce!

99

While his tolerance level was always unbelievably high and his consumption of alcohol matched it, now it has caught up with him. He's very ill with multiple problems—heart murmur, high blood pressure, ulcer, kidney infection, enlarged and inflamed liver, malnutrition. I hurt for him; I feel sorry. I wish I could help. I can't because we don't communicate. He can't even look me in the face.

I pray he'll find help and be able finally to accept it, but dear God, I wish I could get some help for my guilt. I know in my heart that I would make the same decision again. The decision was right. I knew it when I made it. But I wish the pain would go away.

Self-forgiveness is a giant step toward burying the pain that will not die. Bitterness helps to keep the pain alive. If it is ever to be laid to rest, the bitter person needs to *forgive the one who caused the pain.*

Bitterness entered Billie's heart when her husband died.

I found out that we didn't have the 100 percent death debt insurance that he had told me we had, but instead just 50 percent. I had been lied to about this and it still hurts.

Death is not the worst thing that can happen, but when it brings so many ill feelings and bitter thoughts, then it's a terrible thing. Being lied to hurt more than if he had just run off and left me. In fact, I felt that death had cheated me of my opportunity to tell him how I felt. He always wanted to spend money and made fun of the fact that my teaching brought in so little to help us out. But if I had not taught as long as I did, I would have no way now of taking care of our debts, and my retirement would not mean very much when that day comes. When the estate settlement was made and the debts were all mine, I was consumed with anger and deeply depressed.

A sense of betrayal makes Billie's pain especially bitter to the taste. There is no greater pain than love that is betrayed, and that may be where forgiveness finds its greatest test. Certainly our Lord Jesus Christ was the victim of unrequited love—betrayed even by those he loved to the point of death. Jesus may have died of a broken heart rather than the physical pain of crucifixion.

It's been 12 years since Billie's husband died. In answer to the question "Do you think you have gotten over it?" she can only answer, "Yes and no."

The toughest petition in the Lord's Prayer—the one we so often slide through tongue-in-cheek—says, "Forgive us our sins as we forgive those who sin against us." Sometimes we just don't *want* to forgive; holding a grudge produces its own grim satisfaction.

The grace of God gently hammers away at our hardness of heart by reminding us of his great love. Forgiveness begins when we stop demanding each other to be more than human. Only God is perfect. Human beings, although forgiven and made clean by the blood of Christ, never attain perfection in this world. So we are assured that Christ loved us and died for us "while we were yet sinners."

Intentionally and unintentionally, we hurt others and need their forgiveness. Even with the best of intentions we find our motives misunderstood. Love is only love when it makes no demands on the other person; but love also gives of itself freely.

We have talked about the need to forgive oneself and to forgive others as though they were separate processes.

Actually they are intertwined. One cannot be separated from the other.

At times our own feelings of guilt are so unbearable that we heap our sins on another person. In bitterness and resentment, we make someone our scapegoat. Georgia has been married longer than a dozen years, but the guilt and bitterness that dominate her relationship with her husband are a result of the sexual experiences they shared before marriage.

> When I came to know the Lord after five years of experiencing hell in our marriage, I felt dirty, cheap. God couldn't love me after what I had done, I thought, and I couldn't forgive myself or forget what I had done. I felt like committing suicide lots of times and I wanted to hurt my husband because "it was all *his* fault!"

Georgia feels that her actions in the past are blocking her enjoyment of lovemaking in the present. She writes openly of both her despair and her hope.

> I have never to this day been able to really enjoy sexual intercourse. I get down lots of times and only God's mercy lifts me up. I don't bear my cross very well. I feel that I'm being cheated. More than anything else in the world, I want to enjoy lovemaking. As I grow in my love for the Lord, I'm beginning to accept my husband, but I have a long ways to go to get rid of all the bitterness and resentment that I have built up inside me!

Georgia points out a common experience on the way to accepting total forgiveness in Christ. Pain may be temporarily increased. Georgia describes her "coming to know the Lord" as the period when she felt most "down." The reason? At that point her image of her "real" self was at its greatest distance from the "ideal" person she wished to be for Christ's sake.

Linnie consumed bitterness in huge doses, keeping her pain alive and well. She has never forgiven the lover who rejected her after they had lived together for a number of years with the promise of marriage to come. After he left, she entered, as she puts it, into a life of "bitter spinsterhood." Note how it colors all her thinking and expectations.

> After I moved in with my mother, I assumed the role of rejected spinster in all of its aspects, no social life, no hopes for the future. In my heart I felt my life could only get worse—a single woman is usually always a social outcast, a threat to the safety of family life. Generally the single person is not invited to social events of any importance. A single person is generally considered a nuisance.

> Widows find this area hard to take and complain a lot; spinsters shrug the situation off, they are used to being rejected and expect it. They are surprised and grateful if anyone is kind to them. Widows usually feel that they still deserve all the love and acceptance and position that they used to have as married women; spinsters expect nothing and treasure any little tidbit that falls their way.

> Well, anyway, to get on with it, I decided my greatest hope lay in death. This world obviously had nothing to offer me, so I began to prepare for death with spiritual renewal because I had not attended church for years.

> Church was a bitter experience for me. Sometimes I left early, weeping at the sight of all the warm, happy families. I felt even more rejected because church is made for family groups. I made many kind and thoughtful friends, but I still felt like an out-

sider. I felt as worthless as ever. It was not the fault
of my friends.

Linnie may be assuming more than her share of responsibility for her feelings of rejection by church folk.
Don't most congregational programs reveal an intense
preoccupation with family life, which virtually guarantees that members who are single, divorced, or widowed
will feel slighted and second-rate? To be married is
held up as "normal" (Are singles "abnormal"?), and the
married person, especially the married woman, is labeled
"fulfilled." Marrieds are described as "complete," a description which infers that singles are "incomplete"
fractions of a whole human being.

As we become increasingly sensitive to the needs of
the over one-third (37%) of our adult population which
is single, pastors will guard against sermon illustrations
which infer that to be single is to be less than whole,
and congregations will strive to incorporate singles
into all aspects of congregational life and leadership.
While Linnie's extreme reaction is by no means characteristic of all singles, many an otherwise well-adjusted
single wilts under the unfunny jokes about "old maids,"
the frantic matchmaking carried on in their behalf by
well-meaning married friends, and church programs
which imply that singleness is somehow against God's
will and therefore wrong.

Linnie's experience in the church effectively gagged
her and bound her to ongoing pain.

> I never brought up my feelings to anyone, of course.
> It would have been the ultimate humiliation. In fact,
> I never discussed with anyone my spinsterhood and
> the grief and humiliation that go with it. A spinster is
> a figure of fun, like the village idiot. Your grief would

generally be considered humorous to the rest of the world.

Dear Linnie, poor Linnie, irritating Linnie! Why didn't she open up to anyone? Are we church folk really *that* unapproachable and judgmental? How did she know she would be rejected? What made her project this image onto everyone she met? What made her believe that her fantasy of what would happen was accurate? Why did she prejudge what others would think or were thinking about her?

Linnie still looks at the world through the eyes of the lover who rejected her and she assumes that the world looks at her with his eyes. Today, more than 20 years after her unhappy love affair, bitterness feeds her pain, sealing it within.

Bitterness also protects her from further pain. By convincing herself that nobody loves her, she can excuse herself for not loving anyone else. Loving is too risky. Hurt once, she's not going to risk getting hurt again. The pain is too great, especially for someone who feels things as keenly as Linnie does, so her protection against further pain is to seal herself off from getting close to another person.

Human love brings with it no guarantees that it will last forever. We take each other on faith. Marin, who felt betrayed and used by her former husband, dared to risk loving again. Two years after her divorce she married a man she had only known a couple months. The risk was even greater "because I was so ready to marry anyone who wanted me." Her life now, she says, is worth the risk. "I am very content and complete with Christ as the head of my life." She confesses that "it took years after we were married and much loving and giving on my husband's part to help make me a trusting, loving, complete person again."

Nan has gone through much the same experience as Marin did in her divorce, but for her that trust has not been restored. Although she wanted as desperately as Marin to have "a male friend tell me that I wasn't a freak, someone who would evaluate me as being okay," she still has not been able to risk another rejection. In spite of "the most craven need to be a married woman, to love and to be loved, I cannot force myself to take the chance. How can I dare risk it again? I don't even date."

Can you sense the rigidity that's settling into Nan's life—the tightness and wall-building? The longer she holds back from trusting, the more inflexible she will become. Rigidly controlling people are more vulnerable to pain than those who have learned to ride with the waves instead of bucking every breaker that rolls into their lives. Letting go of the need to control brings an end to some of the pain.

Parents especially are subject to continuing pain when they cannot free their children to learn from their own mistakes. We parents take our jobs seriously and our added years give us wisdom, we assume. So we try to control our children's decisions, especially when we see them making choices that we know from experience can only lead to harm. Unless the pain is to live with us forever, we must learn to let them go, to let them live their own lives. Easily said, but not so easily done.

Tess learned that lesson when her middle daughter became involved with a man during her first year in college and broke with her parents' value system and beliefs to live with him. He dominated her life completely, Tess writes, and still does, although he keeps on having affairs with many other young women.

There was nothing we could say or do that would change things. She is just now beginning to extricate herself from his control over her and to regain her sense of self-worth. Throughout the long, long ordeal of not knowing what to do and of being uncertain how to handle our feelings, I found release when I learned that I couldn't control anything! What I did or did not do did not seem to matter. I could only love and support her wherever possible without compromising my own values. With the understanding that I did not any longer need to control her life came my own release from the unbearable pain of seeing this beloved child go in such strange and awful paths.

As Tess learned, none of us can control the life of others or make their choices for them, even if they are our own children. Someday they will have to be on their own, taking their own "lumps."

Reversing the usual control relationship, Emily embarked on the painful course of trying to control her father's salvation, and she lives with the pain of not knowing whether she succeeded.

Her father died when she was in her late 20s. All through her childhood she worried about him because he was not a "church-going man." "I don't believe my father was saved. I tried so hard to get him to go to church with me and I wanted to know that he was a believer. But he died so suddenly of a heart attack and I've still got fearful feelings because I'm scared for my father's future. I wish there was some way I could have *made* him believe!"

As Tess found out, release from the pain that has come from a situation we couldn't control only comes when we let go of our own need to control the lives of those around us. Those out-of-control situations come even when we're not making any choices. They are nobody's fault; they are part of the business of living, and they bring continuing pain with their frustrations.

Dagmar found love to be her answer to pain. When her husband of 40 years had a stroke, he lost his speech, and he could not feed himself, walk alone, or take care of his toilet duties. His mind never returned to normal, and much of the time he lives in the events of 50 years ago. Dagmar wants to weep and fight against her "fate." She wonders many times why this happened to a man she knew as very dear.

> I knew that I could not give up hope, even though there was nothing I could do to change the situation. What's going on in his arteries and brain is something I can't control. All I can do is pray that my love will never cease.

> I am confined to long hours at home, but I have had more time to study the Word than I have ever had before. I put my husband to bed by six P.M. and he's up before six A.M. and does not sleep during the day. Bedtimes are especially hard to deal with; he's at his worst then. I hope he will never have to be confined to one room or restrained as he was at one time.

> Yes, I still get discouraged, but I try to bring my anger and discouragement to the Lord and just go on loving my husband.

The pain of loving deeds undone and loving words unspoken carries a special sting. After her daughter's death, Lily wrote:

> I felt like no matter how hard I had tried to be a good mother, I hadn't been good enough. I told her I loved her, but not often enough! I feel very bad

about that (it hurts so much even now), and I feel that I let her down and the Lord, too, because she was my responsibility and I failed her and God miserably.

If Jesus offered her back to us, though, I would have to say, "No, Lord, she's better off with you." But oh, how I would welcome her with open arms and lots of love and I'd tell her I love her *often*. Oh, for a chance to tell her!

Lily and all of you reading these words, be assured that those you loved *know* those things that you wanted to say and that you are even now saying in your heart. The Lord who intercedes for us hears the cries of your heart and makes your love known to those who are with him.

The forgiving and healing grace of God must be allowed to come into all the memories that are keeping pain alive if that pain is ever going to die. "Healing of the memories" is a popular concept today. Agnes Sanford may have been instrumental in shaping it as a process and many others have publicized it in their ministries. I have found it of great help in releasing people from the pain attached to particular memories.

Where does pain center in your memory? Sit back and relax for a moment, close your eyes, and experience the tension flowing out of your body, out through your fingertips and toes. Feel yourself relaxing. Breathe in deeply, mindful of the fact that God's Spirit comes as the wind—filling you with peace, power, forgiveness, and blessed relaxation. Now recall that memory which always brings with it familiar feelings of shame, guilt, self-loathing, regret. Feel again all the heartache associated with it, the hurt, the feelings of being unloved and uncared for. Feel that sense of rejection that causes your stomach to constrict and a lump to form in your throat.

Feel your heart throbbing with the sorrow of that memory.

Hold it in your mind as a picture. Now into that memory see Jesus walking, bringing love and forgiveness. Feel the touch of his hand on you and see his eyes encompass the whole scene lovingly. Hear his voice say to you, "Daughter, your sins are forgiven. Be healed. Go in peace and wholeness. Your pain is taken away."

You are set free forever from the pain of that memory. Whenever the accusing voice is heard inside you again, you can simply say, "But all of that is forgiven. Jesus Christ was there at that moment. He knows. He understands. He has forgiven me. The memory has no more power over me. The pain is gone." The next time the memory comes you will see it only as a picture in your mind, but you will no longer feel its sting.

Mary's marriage was being destroyed because of her painful memories of an incestuous father who deserted the family while she was still a young girl. But she had transferred the guilt from those memories to her husband and he became the scapegoat for her anger and hostility. We spent a Sunday afternoon sorting out those memories, identifying them and bringing the loving forgiveness of the Lord into them. Two weeks later a letter came from Mary.

> Remember the door that I mentioned was opened into my poor soul the day we were with you? There has been a veritable parade of "horny toads" slinking out of my memory through that door for weeks.
>
> These are the most exciting and confirming days, I believe, of my life! The miraculous healing stream of God in our lives in what he is doing and the way he is doing it "blows my mind." I feel like I just got married to a very special man. Never would I have dreamed after 25 years that this could be my expe-

rience. I don't yet understand with my intellect but from the time we left your house I have not seen him with the same eyes.

Just briefly I'll mention the next "biggie." For years I've wondered what I was doing wrong and why I seemed to alienate my children from me (and, of course, others). Now I've seen it! That ugly defensive spirit, towering in all its false splendor, clothed in moral righteousness, spewing out truth and good works, but not daring to be exposed for what it really was. But they knew it was there disguised as love. They just didn't know what to name it.

And they have suffered. All three of them bear the marks of my defensive spirit. The Lord is guiding and giving opportunity for me to share what I'm seeing and learning and to ask forgiveness. The spinoff means the surfacing of other garbage and I'm trusting that God will finish me off.

But you know, even though my life has been a lot of garbage in many ways, Jesus has ministered his love to me every minute. He holds me like a little infant and I just snuggle, literally feeling his love absorbing my life. *Every memory is being healed.* I'm truly experiencing his unconditional love, independent of my performance.

We are not afraid now of the future. He is the future as well as the past. The world and the church are ready but not much can happen anywhere until Kingdom people are healed. I know.

The undercurrent of pain may always remain like the solo of the oboist, even when the swells and crescendos of the orchestra almost hide its throb. Let it be there reminding you of the healing power of God, who has taken away its sting in order to release it as a creative force in your life.

Your new birth beyond crisis has its accompaniment of pain, as does all birth. But that's what it takes to create new life.

Something to think about

How long has it taken you to learn to live with your pain?

Where does it come from—unaccepted forgiveness? An unforgiving and bitter spirit? The need to control? Unhealed memories? Or is it creative pain? How can you tell?

What are your feelings now as you look back?

How has the pain that will not die enriched your life?

7

THE REBORN SELF

> dreams with happy endings
> come to mind
> gentle veils sifting out
> the pain which can turn
> those same dreams to nightmares
> it is blessed relief
> for who could bear
> the tons of tears shed
> in our minds
> when our hearts are numb?

Susan sent me poems written during her moments of "tightroping along the edge." Chris shared the songs she had received as a gift from God during her friendship-crisis. Hundreds of autobiographical letters, copies of pages from private journals, and paintings produced out of pain have been sent to me.

Crisis raises us out of the ashes of all that we used to be into a new life. In Chapter 1 I described crisis as tearing life in two with its taloned claws. Those two halves of life can never be welded together again. What was before bleeds to death and part of us is forever buried with it.

But on this side of crisis, trembling new life springs forth, formed out of the ashes of the old. For a time, all is without form and void, but as the Spirit of God broods over the chaos of our troubled private world, a new creation comes forth—the reborn self that is me!

That reborn self is a creative new person out of whom flows a variety of new forms of expression. The chaos produced by crisis demands a reworking of our lives, a rethinking of our beliefs, a redefining of our selves and our relationships. All of the creative potential which was dammed up by the crisis now is channeled out as creative energy, actively working to make sense out of the crisis.

The person in crisis is on the edge of unknown territory. Her world has become a psychodrama played on a stage where some of the characters have disappeared or changed roles or rewritten the script. Her lines are all wrong after years of saying them the same way in the same role. She must create a new part for herself, rewrite the lines to fit the new plot, work out new stage "business" to keep her hands and body moving as she rehearses her new role.

Who am I? Where did the familiar actors go? Don't I have anything to say about the plot?

Above all, I want to talk to the Director! Why is he letting all these changes take place in my life? Who's in charge on life's stage, anyway?

Poets, writers, artists, speakers are the products of crisis. To create is to step into unknown territory where one has never been before. Beyond their crises, the women on these pages became more than the sum of all the parts of the crisis experience. They are *new creations*.

Some of their descriptions of their new "being" help us see the larger dimensions of their newness. Tina, admitting to some undercurrent of sadness over her divorce, nevertheless exults, "I feel like a butterfly—emerged from a cocoon. A whole new world has opened for me!"

Monica, 11 years after her breakdown, rejoices:

> I lost the battle but won the victory. I have discovered the love and promises of God in ways I never knew before. I hear God promising me that I will never be left an orphan—that I will always know God's presence. I can truly say now that I love God, trust God and give God thanks and praise in a way I never could have unless I had gone through all of what happened to me.

Twelve years after she was wrongfully ousted from her job as college dean of women, Liz is able to say:

> Each year has been better. Today my peace is very real, for I feel that God has worked out everything for good in my life. I am really free! For the first time in my Christian life I know what it is to let go and let God, and what faith is all about. That seeming tragedy in my life set me free to be a real person, released from the 'tin god' of my position.

So the comments go on and on—"I am set free!" "I praise God for my crisis!" "I'm a stronger person for having lived through this!" "I have seen life in new ways since it all happened!" This note of resurrection joy sounds from most women who told their crisis stories.

How does crisis become power? How is pain transformed into strength?

Crisis forces an encounter with life's basic realities. Against our will, crisis engages us in hand-to-hand combat with our own mortality. The either/or nature of crisis involves wrestling with such basic choices as, either I live or die, either I cope or go insane, either I find out who I am or I disintegrate. We face death in all of its forms—death of love, death of innocence, death of trust, death of hope, death of loved ones, death of marriage, death of life itself.

Without this kind of in-depth encounter with the ultimate questions of existence, we can only live our lives on a very shallow plane, making naive assumptions about right and wrong, good and evil, heaven and hell, God and Satan. Answers come easily because we have never had to struggle with the questions in our own experience. Persons who give glib answers to such questions as Why do the righteous suffer? or Was it God's will that this person died in an accident? usually have never had a crisis encounter.

Individuals who struggle with the meaning of existence lose some of the smug assurance that characterizes the naive pre-crisis state. They move from sweeping global generalizations about God's will for everybody to the smaller, more realistic understandings they have discovered in their own experiences.

But while they are less sure of themselves and their own assumptions, they are more sure than ever before that God is real, active, and lovingly present in their lives. The answers they have found fit their own lives, but they are reluctant to impose those answers on others. They only share them in the hope that they will encourage others to work through their own pain.

The value of working through one's own pain is affirmed. "The struggle was worth it" runs as a refrain

118

through the stories, "because without it I wouldn't be what I am today."

I hate to see others suffer. I see that as a weakness in me because it probably indicates that I'm afraid their pain will recall all the pain that lives in me. So I have been guilty of trying to take everyone's tears away, to stop their crying and heal their wounds—prematurely. I wonder how many butterflies I've killed by tearing off their cocoons too soon and denying them the struggle that makes their wings strong enough to fly.

I try to watch myself now and exercise restraint, because I have come to believe that the strength and power to live a joyous life comes only through a painful encounter with death, life's basic reality. Life and its struggles have no meaning if death is the end of it all. Even though we hear answers from others, preached in sermons and shared in books, when it comes to wrestling with death, each one of us has to "reinvent the wheel" in our own pain and agony. Sometimes the pain goes on for years. It's during that time that we need all the help we can get as God's Spirit works through promises, prayers, and people.

Inga, torn from her family after 31 years of marriage, says, "For almost five years I spent days and hours praying for guidance, strength, and help. I literally became a recluse. I felt there was no way in my bewilderment and confusion that I could endure the shattering of all my idealistic dreams. The only way I could survive was by constant prayer and the claiming of God's promises."

What if some "helpful" person came along before those five years of painful encounter with the death of dreams were up and tried to cut short those days of prayer and aloneness with God? A wise man once said "there is a time to weep" and joy only comes when the days of weeping have run their course.

Those who experience ultimate victory do so to the degree that they have been absorbed in the battle. Remember all those statements about "putting the burden on God," "letting go and letting God," "releasing it into God's hands"? *But there had to be total absorption in the struggle before the release came!* And release is in direct proportion to the tightness with which the mainspring of the struggle is wound.

The account of the Apostle Paul's conversion is the most dramatic record of that kind of experience in the New Testament. His struggle to know God involved him in murderous intent toward all believers in Jesus Christ. His opposition to them was violent. It was at the height (or depth) of his absorption in carrying out his task that the Spirit broke through, spinning him around and setting him on the very course he was resisting.

At the moment of intense absorption with finding the answer beyond the crisis, women see the God who is *for* them! Even while they are shaking their fists at heaven and crying against their abandonment to a hostile fate, God is revealed as the Resurrected One who turns death into life. They are free at last! Joy replaces anxiety and fear is transformed into ecstasy!

To express this joy and ecstasy, words of praise pour forth spontaneously from lip and pen, similar to Mary's ecstatic song, "My soul magnifies the Lord, and my spirit rejoices in God my Savior, for he has regarded the low estate of his handmaiden" (Luke 1:46-48).

In the encounter with death, the struggler with crisis discovers a greater reality in the resurrection to newness of life.

Crisis also enables us to communicate on a deeper level. The need to express our feelings during the traumas of crisis creates a new climate for communication. We have stood before God and others with all our weaknesses and shameful feelings revealed. Crisis rendered us naked and despised in our own eyes. Others have seen us as we really are in our suffering and need. There is nothing left to hide.

People who have risked revealing their secrets and have discovered that the risk paid off in deeper understanding from others, no longer fear self-disclosure. I have found that they move much more readily from the usual superficial social chatter to talking about those subjects which encourage others to be less defensive and guarded. Intimacy and spiritual contact become possible earlier in the relationship.

Haven't you talked to people as boring as the Pharisee whose prayers consisting of long recitations of his virtues and credentials? Talking about other people and their faults or about our own roles and accomplishments reveals a fear of people finding out what we are really like. But those who have weathered crisis have had a glimpse into their own private hell and the possibility of a world without the presence of a loving God. They seldom go back to the old social pretenses.

The new openness transforms interpersonal relationships. When a young pastor's wife found out that her husband had had an affair with a woman whom he was counseling, she went through nine months of hell, consumed by jealousy and the pain of rejection. Like Monica, she felt that she could not go to anyone with her problem. Since her husband was her pastor, she felt she couldn't go to another pastor for counseling.

> There was only God, and I poured out everything in prayer. That was a very hard year for my husband and me because we were very distant from each other. Out of my hurt I completely held back from talking to him.

Finally my feelings just exploded eight months later and after a long night of struggling and talking and praying we finally cleared the air of all that we had refused to talk about.

We then agreed on some major ideas: that we could forgive even that much if our love was behind it and that to live a full life we would have to take the risk of getting to know other men and women well enough to fall in love with them. We faced the fact openly that we were both attractive people and that a marriage certificate would never protect us from temptation; we would have to be responsible to God for our actions.

I also got up courage out of my new sense of openness and freedom to confront this other woman (now divorced from her husband) to avoid having to pretend the next time I saw her. I ended up feeling sorry for the woman I had hated, for she seemed to me to have nothing.

Openness with others calls forth open responses from them. This is true not only on a human level. Open communication results in deeper conversation with God. When the Pharisee told God all about his good deeds, do you think he waited for a response from God? But consider the publican praying nearby, who could only beat his breast and confess, "God, be merciful to me a sinner!" That cry comes out of the agony of personal crisis, and the response from God is the deepest we can hear. The publican went home justified, forgiven, restored.

Up against the edge of death in any of its forms, prayer gets down to business. Pleasant petitions and shallow requests give way to the kind of "wrestling with God" that Jacob engaged in. God has seen our writhings in the pit of despair, heard our screams of anger, and watched our hostile actions, so there is nothing to hide any longer. Pretense is discarded like an outgrown garment and we stand spiritually naked and defenseless, only to find ourselves gently clothed in the precious robes of our Lord Jesus Christ.

And God talks back to us. Have you listened? Is that deeper communication part of your prayer life? Greater self-disclosure on our part invites greater self-disclosure from God. Or it may be that we have simply become more sensitive listeners.

Crisis also prepares us for a life of ministry to others.

> Though I suffered more than I have ever suffered before, I have seen the Lord open doors of ministry through this suffering that would never have been open otherwise. I am able now to share the comfort I have received.

That statement is repeated with infinite variations, but always the thrust is toward others rather than toward one's own needs. Those who were preoccupied with their own concerns before the crisis now reach out to others in loving concern. They develop an attractiveness which seems to draw others.

This drawing power is a consequence of the joy and strength they reflect. When I asked Marin, "What would you do differently if you could?" she replied, "Isn't it a wonderful gift that we don't have to waste time wondering about that because nothing can, or needs to be, changed. We have to accept it all, good and bad, and each day grow stronger in Christ's love with the counseling of the Holy Spirit. I've learned to live each beautiful day in its entirety. Life really is wonderful!"

As you read that, you probably find yourself wishing you knew someone like Marin to talk to about your crisis. If she has come through her suffering with that kind of joy, you want to know her secret. Apparently many others feel the same way because Marin finds abundant opportunities to exercise her new ministry of support.

But through it all and looking back, I'm thankful that I went through the experience and came to know that Christ's healing hand was real. Now when I talk to God and listen to others, I don't bother to give any advice and speak a lot of meaningless words, but I simply listen. That was one of my weaknesses before. I did a lot of talking but I rarely listened. Now the best way I can be of help to others is by being supportive, letting them talk and hoping to be able in some little way to let them know about the love of Christ that shines at the other end of the tunnel of life's experiences. Praise the Lord that the light is always glowing there even though at times we can't see it!

Sometimes the ministry is not to a woman's liking. It may be thrust on her against her will. Carlyn's crisis brought its own ministry with it.

When I discovered that our six-month-old son was severely retarded, had violent seizures, and probably couldn't see, I felt like God was on vacation. "How could this happen to me?" I cried. Just about the time he was approaching his first birthday and couldn't turn over, crawl, or hold anything in his hands, I couldn't face the sight of another child his age because all of my expectations had died.

Finally, two years ago, I couldn't carry the load any longer and I turned the whole thing over to God. Since that time, Bobby has ceased to be a burden and blesses us each day. He is the Lord's own "special" child and has been a blessing to many. Because of the "mystery" of Bobby, we have entered a totally different spiritual dimension.

The problem has not changed but it has become a blessing. I know that God picked me out for special service to him.

Chris feels that her songs are a way of ministering. She no longer worries about not being a "nurturing" person as she reaches out to others.

I couldn't ache for someone when I didn't know what suffering was myself. I needed to experience that in order to care about another person. Sometimes I feel like quitting and going back to being the carefree, unfeeling person I used to be, but then I read Hebrews 13:3, where it says, "Remember those who are suffering, as though you were suffering as they are."

So now I am encouraging people a lot more verbally, by touch and by writing notes. My conviction now is that I at last have something to give to others, and I've developed my own guidelines for reaching out. Listen to people and accept where they are. Do not always go for change. When a person is unable to handle a situation alone, God will provide someone to help. Sometimes I'm a giver and sometimes a receiver. Jesus supports me; he even uses my mistakes. I need to give without expecting something back. If an idea floats in to help, to give of myself or to support someone—I go ahead and do it.

If I get hurt feelings I will do my best not to withdraw but still think of others and express love to them; think outward not inward, and that's difficult! I sure need Jesus.

After her five years of withdrawal in order to find the God behind her agony, Inga "simply relaxed and accepted God's love," and the doors of ministry flew open for her.

Now my heart is so full of love and joy! God is ever present with me. He has used me to minister to others in so many unbelievable ways! At times I am almost awestruck at things that happen in relation to perfect strangers. When people say how I have encouraged and helped them, I honestly say, "Not I, but Christ through me." In turn they pass on to others the joy and guidance the Lord has given them. It gets to be a beautiful and explosive chain reaction of love and caring!

So the words of the Scripture become flesh again in the lives of those who have persisted in digging out its answers to the "why" of suffering and crisis and have found them in the "how" of ministering. The chain reaction goes on as Romans 5:3-5 outlines it: "More than that, we rejoice in our sufferings, knowing that suffering produces endurance, and endurance produces character, and character produces hope, and hope does not disappoint us, because God's love has been poured into our hearts through the Holy Spirit which has been given to us."

That is the testimony of those who have shared in the writing of this book. Their reward is in that love of God poured into their hearts through the Holy Spirit. In turn they pass it on to you.

Something to think about

Describe your reborn self. How does it differ from the person you used to be?

What new doors of ministry have opened as a result of your reborn self?